ALI NEWTON-TEMPERLEY

# Agency Exits

AGENCY EXITS

*First published by Agency Exits Ltd 2025*



*First edition*

*ISBN: 9781068263705*

*This book was professionally typeset on Reedsy.*
*Find out more at reedsy.com*

# Contents

# Acknowledgments

What a wild ride! I knew writing this book was going to be difficult, but my goodness - the early mornings, late nights and weekends spent bringing *Agency Exits* to life have been something else. There's no way I could have done it without the help of so many incredible people along the way.

First, my husband, Charlie Temperley, who has won many hats throughout this process - sounding board, volunteer editor, chief encourager and everything in between.

There are seven interviewees in this book - all of whom fit me into their busy schedules to share their experiences of selling their agency. I'd hoped we would learn from their challenges and successes, but I discovered so much more. Each brought not only their expertise but also their vulnerability, sharing things that can be difficult for founders to talk about. I thank them as interviewees - and, in many cases, as new friends and even a new business partner. Thank you Luke Tobin, Jack Porter-Smith, Mark Wright, Jon Payne, Dominic McGregor, Tim Cameron-Kitchen and Andrew Bloch. There could be no book without you.

Thank you also to my advance readers, who helped shape the manuscript into what you see now. Your thoughts and ideas made it so much better. Ben Scoggins, Nigel Wilkinson, Jenny Walford, James Howell and my Mum and Dad - I'm grateful for your time and honesty. Phil Treagus-Evans and Ryan Hall also shared their own book experiences and gave me more than one well-timed pep talk - thank you both.

Last but not least, thank you to the Unusual Group team for your support and encouragement along the way.

# Introduction

*"A goal without a plan is just a wish."*
*– Antoine de Saint-Exupéry, Le Petit Prince*

Agencies do better when they're built to sell. Whether and when you sell is up to you. While some founders know from the first day, they would like to sell, others feel they want a business they can work on forever. Regardless of whether the intention is to actually go through with it, businesses that are built to sell create options and opportunities - both for the owner, and the teams that work there. When your agency benefits from you, but isn't dependent on you, *everything gets better.* Systems run smoother. Teams get stronger. Pipelines grow more resilient. And you, the founder, get to breathe again.

I'm not here to glorify selling your agency (although if that's where you're heading, this book will certainly help you get there). My goal with *Agency Exits* is to demystify the journey from stressed-out owner to agency leader with options - including the option to walk away for a meaningful sum.

Let's be honest: it takes a certain kind of person to decide to start a business in the first place, let alone *an agency* of all things! Entrepreneurs already need strength, grit and determination; agencies demand all of that on fast-forward and by the boatload.

And the last few years have been tough. Brutal, in fact. We thought the pandemic would be the hardest chapter, but many of us look back now and realise we came out of that stronger - if a little scarred. Since then we've faced rising costs, ghosting clients, AI disruption, talent shortages, and a market that just won't settle. It's no surprise so many agency leaders are asking: '*Is there another way?*'. For some, that answer to that question is stepping back. For others, it's stepping out entirely.

When I sit down with founders, the conversations are often similar. They tell me they love their business, and they do. They love the team, the momentum, the creativity. But they're also exhausted. They feel stuck in the weeds. The pressure is constant. They love their agency, but somewhere, under all of that, they wonder what it might be like to exit. Or at the very least, to drop into a less hands-on role.

It's often said with some internal conflict. For most founders, the agency is more than a business. It's part of who they are. Years, sometimes decades, of their lives have been invested in it. And yet, when they look ahead, the path from here (tired, firefighting, over-relied upon) to there (valuable, scalable, maybe even sellable) feels foggy at best.

Add into the mix that choosing to sell your business is at once emotional and commercial. While some owners desperately want to escape the stress and responsibility of carrying everyone, many worry about redundancies for their team. Some worry that they'll get a poor deal, or that they'll regret it. And so, what happens? The dream goes back in the drawer, and they soldier on, wondering if things will ever change.

That's why I wrote this book.

The more I work with agencies, the clearer the patterns become - and the more undeniable the difference between those that are just about managing and those that are building sellable value (and getting more sleep at night).

I've seen what happens when agencies make themselves founder-proof. My first experience wasn't as an agency owner, but as someone tasked with making an agency function without its founder. I joined an independent agency where the owner was doing most of the sales, the invoicing, the people management... you already know what this looks like. Then, after a year spent earning my stripes, he asked me to release him from sales and build a scalable sales function.

I now know how many agencies have tried and failed to replace the founder in sales. But I was young, ambitious, and didn't know any better. It consumed me. As Head of Sales, I built a systematised sales team that made the founder completely redundant in new business - and it worked. So well, in fact, that we'd grown to the point that it was time to put directors in place.

As Commercial Director, I managed the agency's revenue, sales, marketing, and account management teams. We more than doubled the agency and reached 80+ staff. The founder was now not just redundant in sales - but across the whole operation. They found their freedom.

And me? I still wasn't done.

I wanted to help more founders achieve the same, which is why I started *The Agency Growth Pad.* Since then, I've worked with agencies across the UK and US, and while every one is different in size, sector, and service, the patterns are consistent. The agencies that thrive are the ones that make themselves less reliant on the founder, and more resilient as a business; the agencies that love, but don't *need*, their founder.

A warning: the process does not happen overnight, and often we must push through painful patches to get to the other side. But there *is* an 'other side'. And there are patterns you can follow to get there.

This book is about those patterns.

You'll hear from seven agency leaders who've built businesses with real value - and, eventually, stepped away. Some sold. Some stayed. Some handed over to their leadership team. All of them had to do the hard work of making themselves less essential - and the business more complete.

Each story is different. But the common thread is that every founder in this book built their agency to be sold. Because doing so gave them freedom - even if they chose not to use it.

You'll hear from seven agency leaders who've done it. Some sold, some stayed, some passed the reins to their team. Every path winds its own way. But the common thread is that they built their agencies to be sellable. That gave them their freedom, even if ultimately they chose not to sell. The stories fill in the missing pieces we don't see in the exit press releases and LinkedIn posts. They show that there's no single path to exit - and that it's not just about the money.

It's about freedom. Optionality. Stability. And building a business that's valuable whether you sell it, scale it, or simply step back.

Let's begin.

* * *

## How to Read This Book

This isn't a theory book. It's a collection of real stories from founders who've built and exited agencies - alongside the lessons you can use to shape your own path.

The interviews focus on three central questions:

## What Makes a Great Founder?

You'll see the mindsets, habits and flaws that shaped these leaders. I studied psychology before I entered the marketing world, and I am fascinated by mindset and what gives people the grit and courage to achieve. Running an agency takes resilience, creativity and determination - and it's often the founder's development that sets the pace for the agency.

## What Makes a Successful Agency?

We'll look at how they positioned, grew and structured their business. You'll see what worked, what didn't, and how they built value beyond themselves to make their agencies attractive to their clients, teams and eventually their acquirers.

## What Makes a Strong Exit?

This is where it comes together. You'll see the timing, negotiations and decisions that defined each exit - and the lessons that will help you when it's your turn.

At the end of each chapter, I have prepared my key takeaways to show you what to do, what to avoid, and how to prepare your own agency for sale.

By the time you reach the end, you'll have three things:

- A clear picture of what it takes to build a sellable agency.
- A checklist to assess how exit-ready your agency is today.
- Practical next steps if you want to prepare now.

This book is designed to be read cover to cover, but you can also dip back in later. If you're wondering about culture, head to Jack's story - *Let Go Of Your Lego.* Curious about negotiation? See Mark's - *You'll Sell It, Drop Dead, or Go Broke.* Looking for a creative deal structure? See Jon - *It's Your Money Or Your Life.* Thinking about valuation? Mark and Luke (*4% of Agencies Sell)* have lessons for you there. Curious about adapting to an AI world or what it's like to go public? Head to Dom's chapter - *Diamonds & Social Chain.*

Above all, remember this: selling an agency isn't about luck. It's about readiness. And readiness starts now.

# I

# Hope Is Not A Strategy

# 1

# Energy, Structure & Sales

I was not like other children. At 8, and bored on a Saturday, I took it upon myself to throw a 'dog show' for the neighbours. Motivated by wanting to earn some pocket money, and to show the neighbours what Vinnie (my tolerant and loving Jack Russell) could really do, I set about planning and drumming up interest. I planned a few different elements - most notably a 'guess how many sweets in the jar' style game, a tiny and uninspiring raffle, and I had planned to charge neighbours for cups of tea - but at the last moment my parents stepped in trying to tell me that was probably, 'Going a bit far'. Next on the list was getting the resources I needed. This began with convincing Dad that, to get the best margins, we really *must* go to Macro, and enlisting my friends Rose and Emily, flyers in hand, to knock on doors to let the neighbours know that tomorrow they were in for a treat. Just an average Saturday really.

The show went well. I made some money, which I split with my friends. I don't remember how much now, but I can't think it was more than a tenner after my tea-selling services had been vetoed. But it was a day where I learned I could make something from very little, and it took three things: energy, selling power and planning.

Many years and 'business Saturdays' later, I am an ex-commercial director, a founder, chief operations officer and founding partner. Still, these principles are central to my business outlook. Why do I tell you this? Because we open with the chapters of Mark Wright and Luke Tobin. A pair of my business heroes, and the interviewees where the energy, selling power and planning and structure of their exits are inescapable and inspiring.

They are the perfect place to start. Their approaches resonated deeply with me, and I learned a lot about the power of planning your exit from day one, and deciding who the ideal buyer for your agency is right from the start - just as you would plan your Ideal Client Profile (ICP) for a marketing campaign. I can't wait to share them with you.

# 2

# You'll Sell It, Drop Dead, Or Go Broke

*"One day, believe it or not, you will exit your business. You will either sell it, drop dead or it will go broke."*
*– Mark Wright*

**Entrepreneur:** Mark Wright
**Exit Type:** Buyout
**Exited Agency:** Climb Online
**Time to Exit:** Year 8
**Exit Multiple:** 8.5x EBITDA
**Exit Value:** Rumoured at £10 million, confirmed at 8 figures
**Employees at Exit:** 130
**Purchaser**: xDNA

When I messaged Mark Wright to see if he'd like to be interviewed for *Agency Exits*, I honestly didn't know if I'd hear back. As a multiple business owner, business partner to Lord Alan Sugar, and a winner of *The Apprentice*. I figured there was only a slim chance he'd be reading his LinkedIn DMs - fortunately he was *(which is actually even more miraculous than you may at first realise. You'll see why during the interview).*

We set up a call to run through everything - and he arrived in his pilot uniform. He'd just stepped off one of the training planes belonging to his flight school, WrightOn Aviation. Based on the Gold Coast of Australia, it is just one of the 20+ businesses Mark now owns or advises.

Mark's story began unusually compared to most. He came to London from Australia intending to backpack, but after a short stay, decided to move into the city and take on the high prices in London. Less than a year later, he applied for *The Apprentice.* After beating thousands of contestants, Lord Sugar pointed towards him and said the famous words: 'You're hired!'.

As Lord Sugar's business partner, Mark received a masterclass in negotiation and building businesses to sell. It was fascinating listening to the lessons he'd learned. He considers the opportunity to learn from the self-made billionaire life-changing, and not always in the ways he'd expected. Mark had originally thought it was Lord Sugar's investment he needed. But it soon became clear that the mentorship, accountability and discipline were just as, if not more, valuable.

Mark's agency, Climb Online, was a 50:50 joint venture with Lord Sugar. It reached over £4 million in revenue in its second year and was acquired by the global digital agency group xDNA in 2022 for a rumoured sum of £10 million (according to *The Sun Online*). His acquisition marked the first successful exit of any *Apprentice* winner, and before that, Climb Online was already considered one of the most successful businesses ever launched by a contestant.

I wrote *Agency Exits* for founders who want their agency to be less dependent on them, whether that's with an exit in mind, or simply to grow a better business. While Mark's story with Lord Sugar isn't one that can easily be replicated, speaking with him offered excellent insight into how the pair took the agency from an idea to an 8-figure exit. Along the way, Mark shared the impact and lessons from the tutelage he received from one of the richest people in the UK.

The themes in Mark's story reflect the challenges I hear from agency owners all the time: the balancing act between fast revenue and needing to only take the right clients, finding and trusting the right people to help, handing over the sales function, and identifying the most profitable growth routes.

Solving those challenges was a big part of how Mark made his agency exit ready and could command a much higher than average multiple. Most notably, both he and Lord Sugar designed the agency for sale from day one. Mark cites this as one of the key reasons for the business's growth, and for keeping him focused.

Here is his story.

* * *

## The Entrepreneur

### Origins

*Ali: To get us started, tell us how your career began.*

*Mark:* I'm sitting where it all started, in my parent's house in New South Wales, Australia. I'm from the Australian countryside, and my mum and dad own small businesses. My mum's a hairdresser and owns salons, and my dad is a mechanic and owns car garages.

Even as a young boy, people asked me what made me want to be successful and what made me want to run my own business (because you need to be a bit crazy to run your own business). But I didn't know any other way! Every day at the dinner table, there was talk about how much we should pay employees, what price to put on products, and all of this sort of stuff. You're a product of your environment, and it was ingrained in me from a young age because it was all I heard for 17 years. So it made sense that I would go into business later on. But when I left school, I didn't know what I wanted to do career-wise. I found digital marketing by accident. I'd always had a passion for sport, being healthy, working out, and playing football.

I tried lots of different careers before working as the sales and marketing manager for a personal training college. The college had fallen on hard times, so we were looking for ways to increase its visibility. I started teaching myself about building websites, and doing SEO and PPC. And the company went from tiny sales to in the multi-millions! They were making hundreds of thousands of dollars a month just from keywords changing position and changes I'd made on the website. I could see the impact it was making on businesses when it was done correctly.

I quickly realised that most people didn't understand digital marketing. Most people, particularly business owners, didn't understand how much they could change their business by getting it right. So, for the first time in my life, I had a lightbulb moment of 'This is what I'm meant to do! It doesn't feel like work. I'm really good at it, and it can make a fucking massive impact'. So I fell into this career purely by luck and discovering I was good at it.

Then, like most Aussies, I went backpacking in Europe. I got stuck in the UK and I was broke as flat as a pancake working at a digital marketing agency when one of my friends suggested I go with him to the try-outs of *The Apprentice*. I hadn't heard of the TV show. Also, I hadn't heard of Lord Sugar; he hates it when I say that.

I was one of 75,000 people who tried out for series 10, and I made it into the final 20 selected to go on the show. I was the first Australian winner, and I became Lord Sugar's business partner in 2014. He invested £250,000 in Climb Online, and we worked together for eight and a half years as business partners. It became the most successful business to be founded by an Apprentice winner, and the first one to complete a third-party exit.

There was a lot of turbulence in the digital marketing industry, but Climb Online made me the fortune that I now invest in 20 or so businesses. It taught me so much about running a business, managing people, selecting people, how to price products, and how to do everything. I was a young boy of 24 when I won, and I was an old man of 34 when I exited. I'm so grateful for all the experience, good and bad, because it made me the man, father, and businessman I am today. It's also been truly unbelievable how much impact it has had on the lives and jobs of many.

*Ali: Tell us about the moment after you became business partners with one of the richest men in the UK, who you previously hadn't heard of. What happened the day after you won?*

*Mark:* The most shocking thing to me is how hands-on Lord Sugar was. He said, 'You're going to be my business partner'. And I said, 'Great. What does that mean?'. I'd heard rumours I'd be sitting in a shed in Essex with his team, but that I'd never see him again. I would have accepted that if I'm honest.

It wasn't like that at all. It was instantaneous, with no gap before entering the pressure cooker of working with him. Previously he'd been watching 20 contestants, but now that I'd won, I'd have 100% of his focus. The day after he was WhatsApping me, 'Hey, can you come around to my flat?'. I thought it was pretty cool that Lord Sugar was WhatsApping me. I got there, and he started grilling me, saying, 'Tell me about digital marketing. Have we thought about the website yet?'. We spent the day reconfiguring the business plan. He made it clear what he was happy with, and what he wasn't. We set my starting salary and then while I was sitting there, he transferred me the £250,000.

The other thing is Lord Sugar has an incredible memory where he remembers everything you've ever said. He'd say things like, 'In episode three you said you would do X'. He would remember things I didn't, even years later. So I had to back up all the bullshit I had said on the TV show.

When the TV show aired and the secret was out, I became semi-famous at the same time as being initiated into this new partnership. So I would walk to a meeting with him, and people would stop me for selfies, telling me about their business or offering me products. So there was a lot of pressure from Lord Sugar quickly, and at the same time my new public profile dawned on me.

It was a lot of pressure for a 24-year-old, which I dealt with as best I could. What I didn't expect in the first six months was the negative stance from the digital marketing community. They really didn't like me, particularly the SEO companies. They came out writing negative reviews and blog posts, creating videos on YouTube about how I knew nothing about SEO and was just a glorified salesman, how I'm a shame on the industry and how someone with more technical ability should have won it. It was an enormous concern to Lord Sugar's PR people, so they arranged for me to speak at Brighton SEO. I got booed onto the stage. I've been booed off a stage before, but not walking onto one. So that was a different experience. Then, when we put our website live and someone DOS attacked it and crashed the server. Lord Sugar had been with that hosting company for 30 years, but when that attack happened, they deleted him as a client, along with all of his companies. He was not impressed. It was all coming at me, but I hadn't done anything. It was the enormous profile of the show that provoked a lot of jealousy from these people. Each day was pretty difficult. But if I had to go back and do it all again, I'd still open that door.

## Mindset

*Ali: 75,000 people entered The Apprentice in your year. They were all going for this one role opportunity. If you don't* win, *you come out with some exposure, but otherwise pretty much nothing. What made you think you were going to be the one to win it?*

*Mark:* I've always had what could be called 'main character syndrome'. I always thought I would do something special in my career. If you don't believe it, it's never going to happen, and if you don't believe in yourself, you can't ask your customers or staff to believe in you. All jokes aside, I had this feeling from the moment I put in the application to the day I went to the try out. I've never had another feeling like it at any other time in business. The feeling was that I was in the right place, at the right time, and it was for me. I could see myself as the winner. Not to get too airy-fairy, but I really felt the opportunity was right, and I was certain within myself that I was going to win. I can't explain it any other way.

I was getting through each level of the try-outs, beating thousands of people at a time, and I was quite nonchalant about it. I was like, 'Yeah, of course the winner is right here!' I've had many other opportunities in my life, some quite sizeable, but I have never felt the same as I did in that process.

Warren Buffett says that in your career you get three trips to the buffet, and that was my first one. I think they come at all different times and in all different shapes and sizes, and when they do, you need to recognise them and grab them with both hands. It was just my time.

*Ali: Mindset is a huge thing. We'll get on to negotiations later, but I'm curious about your thinking on mindset and how you approach your day? Ultimately, I think if you've got your mind made up that it's going to* happen;

*you have an advantage going into a negotiation against someone who's not sure?*

*Mark:* I wouldn't want to negotiate against me. That's for damn sure.

I believe mindset is 95% of the battle in all things. Mindset, resilience and mental toughness have given me the strength to do what I have. What I lack in mental acuity, I make up for in mental strength, and there's a lot to make up for, let me tell you! I'm not the sharpest tool in the shed in terms of academia. I did terribly at school. I never went to university except to chase the girls. So I wasn't an academic guy, but I'm tough as old boots and I can handle stress. I always believe I'm going to get the outcome, and that has served me well.

When I'm buying and selling businesses, it's about who blinks first and who's got the bottle. The toughest person in the room wins the deal. Lord Sugar was my old sparring partner, and he is the master. He's really got an instinct for it. It's something you almost can't teach, but you can learn through mentoring and experience. I would say that I didn't start out this way. I've crafted it through watching great business people and through exercise and pushing my body and my mind. I've sat next to great people and thought, 'Far out! That was tough'. I've lost some deals too. I hate losing, but I'm not immune to it. It's taught me how to cope with the stress and pressure of defeat and how to be better in the next opportunity.

Like everybody else, I'm riddled with self-doubt and constantly questioning, 'Should I be here? Is this right for me? I'm not good enough'. But as the camera and lights go on or as I get on the stage, I have this ability to act. Before I was successful, I used to tell people I was a millionaire. And when I was 19, I couldn't have been further away. I used to wear suits and gold watches, so, to look at me, you would think I was a millionaire, but I wasn't until I was about 25.

I have always acted as if the future is inevitable. And even though in private I question myself and stress and worry, I have the ability to say; I feel I'm feeling all that, but I'm going to do this pitch anyway and I'm going to win. Lord Sugar says that I've got a tough ruthlessness to me that he likes. I think he could see that I am a good salesman and that I believed I was going to be successful.

*Ali: What skills do you have that made you right for leading a successful agency?*

*Mark:* My biggest skill was my salesmanship. I came from a business development background and digital marketing sales. So, I always knew I could go out and get us a new customer, which was pretty bloody important. Overall, as a managing director and as a leader, I've always been a great visionary. My ultimate gift as a CEO or creator of businesses is that I can create a vision that I believe in and I'm able to get everyone on board and moving in the same direction. It took me a long time to understand that that was my gift, because I always thought it was digital marketing. But with a gun to my head, I would say my true pillars of success are my ability to cultivate motivation and vision for the company and a great sales force.

*Ali: I see this quite a lot with agency founders. They're often good at* sales, *and in the early* days, *they learn it because they have no choice but* to *get business through the door.*

*Mark:* The better you are at selling, the better you are at business. There is no way you can convince me otherwise. There are a lot of digital marketing agencies that are dormant in Companies House that had great technical people who couldn't sell. If you can't communicate how good you are at what you do, you will not sign anyone up.

* * *

# Building The Agency

## Development

*Ali: Tell us about Climb Online and how it evolved into a successful agency.*

*Mark:* Not many people know this, but my original business plan looked more like GoDaddy. It wasn't a digital marketing agency; it was a website portal where you could do hosting, domain names, SEO, PPC, design, etc. When I presented it to Claude Littner, he said, 'There are too many products. It will cost way more than £250,000, and it's too big for you on your own'. He asked me, 'Which two services do you do best?'. I said, 'SEO and PPC'. He said, 'So that's your business'.

That was probably the best piece of advice I got from *The Apprentice* experience. I was very naïve then, and I have since learned that one of the fundamental mistakes most agencies make is coming to market with too many products. They confuse themselves and their customers. If you're in a restaurant with 900 things on the menu, you get overwhelmed, and the restaurant has to figure out storage and shove everything in the freezer. A digital marketing agency is better if you specialise. You produce a better type of employee, a better product and it's easier to service overall.

We started as a PPC and SEO agency for small businesses. Over time, we evolved into a performance-based digital marketing agency that was relatively full service. We covered paid, organic, website development, social media, and creative. We got there through a lot of trial and error, recruitment, and customer growth and retention. As clients requested more services, we tried to add them to the agency.

Our core products were always social media, paid and organic, and that really drove most of the revenue and brand of the business. You can do a great job of doing their Google ads, but it doesn't matter if the customer doesn't know about it and the results. We had a lot of times when we dropped the website development or creative for a client because I didn't feel we could offer it at the right level. I found the quality of the individuals you hire and retain to be imperative to the success of the agency because it's a consumer success model where you're offering a service at the end of the day. So everything is tied to the service level, the communication quality, and the delivery of the product - you have to get it all right.

*Ali: Earlier you talked about specialisation. You had 6 departments across Creative, Web Development, SEO, PPC, Social Media and Email marketing. Would you do that differently now?*

*Mark:* If I had my time again, I would have SEO, social media, and email. That is it. Websites are the worst things I've ever touched. There are 3 different things: what is in your mind, in their minds and what is possible with their budget. Everyone wants to look like a global player, but has a tiny budget. There are so many moving parts, and I found web developers very difficult to deal with. So you end up with this environment where communication is difficult, delivery is difficult, and it always takes five times longer than everyone thinks it should. I also had a design department and a web development department that completely hated each other, and I always thought I could solve it. I bought a website agency to solve it, but I realised it was a broken environment and that I was wasting a lot of time and money that could be spent in other areas that were more scalable and profitable. So I would like to never think about websites again on any day in my life.

## Growth

*Ali: What did your growth look like?*

*Mark:* I did it all wrong initially, and I had a couple of issues, which will be different from other agencies. When Climb Online went on the telly, we became well known, and we were getting thousands of enquiries. We had 4,000 inbound leads in the first week. It was coming from all angles, and much of it was garbage. Most people just wanted to meet the guy from *The Apprentice* or Lord Sugar, or to pitch us some horse crap idea. There was a lot of time wasted chasing leads that were not a fit or who couldn't afford us. So, I learned a lesson there.

I didn't understand that not every customer was a good customer. My staff used to get very frustrated because I would take on anything. If it looked like a customer, smelt like a customer, and would pay an invoice, I would bring them on board. A lot of the early customer churn we had was because we brought in business that we could never get results for. That was part of my learning process as well. I'm a very optimistic person, so I always genuinely thought I could get results for them. I never knowingly thought that I wouldn't. But my optimism led me into industries that had performed poorly on PPC, or had high CPLs with low budgets, or had a poor website. I learned quickly that if the client has a bad website with poor assets and a low budget, it's a poor performance mix that will not work.

We also had a lot of clients churn early on because I had been cheap in the hiring process. I was getting low-skilled folks and too many customers on low budgets. We finished our first year with 600+ customers and a turnover of £1.9 million. When I sold the business, we only had 48 clients, and the turnover and profits were through the roof. I figured out through a lot of bashing my head into a brick wall that: good people + right customers on the right budget = success. I'm oversimplifying it, but those are the three ingredients of an agency. When I started, I had thought naively that loads of staff and a massive turnover would mean I was a successful businessperson. I thought that if I could tell someone we were turning over £20 million and that I had 900 staff, it would mean that I, and my agency, were really successful. But that's not right at all. It's about how much you are making in profit, who your customers are and how much they are spending.

Lord Sugar used to say to me ad nauseam, 'Mark, turnover is vanity and profit is sanity'. He'd say it over and over, and I'd say, 'Yes, I get it', and he'd say, ' No, you're not getting it'. Ultimately, I think it is the truth. If you focus on quality and put your price up, you'll have fewer campaigns and staff, but you'll also have fewer headaches. You'll provide a better level of service, and you'll make more money. The vanity element really cost me early on.

*Ali: So what did you do to change it?*

*Mark:* I was one very lucky bastard. To give myself some credit, I've always been very open to feedback. I have Lord Sugar as a mentor, and I also pay people for mentoring who are both within marketing and other successful industries. I was always transparent about things that were going wrong in my business. Quite early on, a couple of my mentors said, 'You have far too many customers. Your employees are horrendously low paid, so are they the right calibre?'. I had heard that enough, and I was seeing the results of it, and I realised they might be right. So I made the changes and raised the minimum spend for customers and the requirements they needed to meet in terms of website product quality, and their offering. Then I started bringing in higher-level employees. It took about 18 months, but the results were like night and day.

*Ali: It's a brave decision to make, because as a founder you also look at the revenue and question whether you really want to turn a lead away. You have to really focus on your longer-term goal to get through troughs.*

*Mark:* It hit me in the pocket the hardest. It cost me almost one full year of profits while we made the transition. We were profitable, and I was making pretty decent money before that, but I knew the mechanics were wrong and it was a pretty shit business. So there was a lot of pain, and I had to take most of it financially. We had to change some employees too, so there was also emotional pain. But the environment improved so much.

I have to give credit to some of my leadership team, who were pushing for it for quite some time. I needed to learn the lesson myself as the end decision maker. The key thing I've learned as I've got older is to leave my ego at the door. I've hired great people around me for advice. If I don't listen to that advice, there's no point in having those people around. Particularly if they're all giving similar advice - it's likely it's going to be the truth! There were some people in my leadership team where I disagreed with 90% of the things that they said. But I kept them to give me a different view and feedback, so I knew I had the full picture when I was making decisions.

*Ali: You mentioned you had a tough time with critics. How did you build credibility for the agency?*

*Mark:* Credibility is fundamental because people don't buy from you until they trust you. It's the most important thing in the sales and marketing process. It's important to differentiate too. McDonald's doesn't sell burgers - it's called a McDonald's Big Mac. Climb Online didn't sell SEO; we called it Organic Climber. I was always adamant that our products needed names. These little things create a brand

and confidence. Lord Alan Sugar was very important. Going on *The Apprentice* was very important. But I did all of that stuff because when I started in this game, I couldn't get a meeting with a carpet shop! I would walk in and say, 'Can I talk to you about PPC?', and they'd say, 'We've had 19 emails this morning. You're literally the 20th person to come and talk about digital marketing'.

That got me thinking about how I could differentiate myself, and I saw my competitors were wearing ripped jeans and t-shirts. So, I wondered what if my folks dressed smarter and wore uniforms? All of our staff wore branded uniforms. It's very rare you'll see me without my branded wear because I'm my own ambassador 24-7. If I don't believe in the business, who will? I don't want to wear Louis Vuitton because I don't own his business! I own this one!

I also wondered what would happen if I went on *The Apprentice*? The biggest issue in digital marketing is trust. Everyone's being ripped off by someone who told them they were going to be number one on Google. But Lord Sugar is pretty trustworthy.

So I've always tried to put myself out there and do things. For example, it's night here in Australia, and I'm doing a book with you. I've been relentless in that pursuit throughout my entire career. I'm my own best promoter, and that helps create confidence in all of my businesses and my brand as an entrepreneur. That then washes down into the business community I invest in or own.

*Ali: How did you build your team?*

*Mark:* I didn't do any of the hiring, and that was important because I'm a very old-school, old-fashioned person. You go to the office; you wear your uniform, you're shaved, you finish late; you work until the job's done, sort of old-fashioned, hence why Lord Sugar likes me. I'm all the wrong stuff for today's work environment, and I understand that.

So I have people who work well in today's environment who keep me as far away from the hiring process as possible.

Our HR department would do all of it. I never got involved, and we won all these amazing awards for our culture because I employed people who could build that for us. I had to sign off on all the policies, and I disagreed with much of it, but the great people I hired were advising me on the best way forward. So I signed them off, we won all these awards and sold the business for a bloody fortune. So, it was probably good advice.

*Ali: It takes a lot of trust and security in yourself to sign off on things you disagree with and to keep people around when they disagree with you in a lot of situations. How did you get comfortable letting go and trusting them, particularly when it wasn't you that hired them in the first place?*

*Mark:* Why did you create a business? To make money. If your business is improving and making more money as a result, then the right decisions are being made. If I'm listening to feedback, and actioning advice, and the results are getting better - I continue on that trajectory. My ego stays at the door until the results go down. Then I get to use my lovely ego. So, I always used the business success metrics as the driver of whether I should beat people over the head or listen - because the numbers don't lie.

I met one of my old team members in Germany for lunch last week, and he said that I have a unique ability to make people work way harder than they've ever worked before and to make them take huge risks and take ownership. I think that comes back to creating the vision and goals, and tying people to the numbers. If you do that, you have this recipe for everyone to be trying really hard. When you hire high-quality staff and give them responsibility, they end up policing out the baddies themselves. They'll say, 'This fellow over here isn't very good. He's not pulling his weight. He's not helping us with proposals. He needs to go', or 'This woman is bloody awesome! More of her!'.

*Ali: Without people you can trust making good decisions, you can't stop leaning over their shoulders and there is no scalability. Many of the agencies I work with want to move away from founder-only sales because it's a scalability point, but also an exit point. It's a tough one for many of them* because, *like you, they know how to sell their services very well! How did that journey go for you?*

*Mark:* Exactly right. Through a lot of nagging from my inner circle early on, I built out a sales team. We had a phrase in our business: 'If you got hit by the number six bus, what happens tomorrow?'. If no one else knows what to do and it has a huge business impact, then holy shit, we have to fix it! If I'd got hit by the bus at the start, we wouldn't have had a business. So each day we worked to replace me.

The last thing to go was sales because I enjoyed it, and I was good at it. When I sold my agency at a ridiculous multiple of 8.5x, one of the major catalysts was that I wasn't doing any of the selling. I hadn't sold a deal in donkey's years. I didn't even know how to create a proposal or where the software was. I became so relaxed about it I was completely useless in the process by the end.

Like you said, that's not an overnight process. You need a really good number two and to hand it over very slowly. My number two shadowed me for six months, which was a pretty painful process for them. But they shadowed me until they were as good, if not better than me, and I sent them on their merry way. Guess what? They produced better results than me. Then they became my sales manager and trained the next one and the next until I had 12 salespeople, and half of them were the same standard as me.

The worst lie a business owner tells themselves is that they can do it better than anyone else. It's the biggest lie in the agency startup world. You should train someone to do it better than you, because they can - you just don't like to hear it. Despite saying all of that, I still think I'm better at it than anyone! But I understood that if I ever wanted to leave and sell on my five-year plan, I couldn't be the chief salesperson.

Being an owner is stressful because you've got to pay rent, wages, and bills, and the only thing that brings money in is your sales. Who else can you trust to score the goals more than the star player, the owner? But how long can that go on before it's just exhausting? If you've got a family or pets or a partner, you become an insufferable person because you're always on the phone or checking your email or doing a proposal late at night. In the first two years, I didn't go to bed before midnight, and even then there wasn't a lot of sleep. It wasn't that I was doing big tasks; it was that I was doing too many.

* * *

# The Exit

## Preparation

*Ali: Did you always think you would exit one day?*

*Mark:* Lord Sugar put it in my head right from day one. He said, 'Right, when are we selling this thing?'. I was thinking, 'Oh my god, I haven't even created a letterhead and we're talking about this!'. He instilled in me that whenever you buy or invest in a business, you start with the end in mind so that you create a better business. You'll have better processes, better documentation, and you'll grow people and a structure that means you aren't doing all the work. If you start out thinking, 'We're never going to sell this mother', then you'll end up doing all the work, and create yourself the worst job ever.

*Ali: How did you prepare for the exit?*

*Mark:* Even if we'd never sold Climb Online, our mindset of building for an exit meant it would be a self-sufficient and scalable machine. We actually went further than that and talked about when we would sell it and who to. We tried to make the business look attractive to the people we would try to attract as buyers when the time came.

One of my friends wanted to sell his business to *Virgin*, so he made it look like a *Virgin* company and they bought it. He wanted to sell his second business to *Emirates.* So it was set up to look like them so they would buy it. If you think about this advice regularly, you make decisions that are based around attracting that buyer.

From the first day, we set up Climb Online with a five-year exit window. We sold three years later, in year eight, but I would say that's pretty good going for a startup.

*Ali: How did you know it was the right time to go?*

*Mark:* In the UK, you have this brilliant website called Companies House, and every business must publish its confirmation statement and accounts. So every year your accounts go up, and some people seem to keep a pretty close eye on them. As we started to report what I'd call 'proper numbers', we began to get calls and letters from people who wanted to talk about acquiring us. They were usually other agencies, groups from abroad, VC, and angel investors. There were many people who wanted Lord Sugar to stay so they could be business partners with him. So that was still helping as well. It became clear the interest was heating up, we were doing really well, and I thought, 'Now is a good time to go'. I felt like I had that business figured out, and they always say, 'Go while the going's good because you don't know what tomorrow is going to hold. So go on the way up.'

I also wanted to move. I was about to be a dad, and I'd been gone from Australia for 12 years. So it was the right time for me as the founder. So I took it to the board meeting, and the board agreed unanimously. When we put it on the market, the interest was pretty phenomenal.

## Negotiation

*Ali: Did you use a broker?*

*Mark:* We used a broker in the end because we needed to channel all the interest through one person. Otherwise, there would have been a lot of conversations happening at once, and we wanted to maximise our value. Plus, Lord Sugar is a very successful and wealthy person. So for him, talking about £10 million would be like us spending days negotiating over 50 quid. So we needed someone who had a feel for that end of the market and someone who could negotiate.

Lord Sugar can be cranky. I think if he had been involved in too much of the negotiation, I'd still be working at Climb Online today. It was my first sale, so I was inexperienced, and he was almost too experienced. We needed someone to bring structure and give us information in the correct way, so we used a broker.

*Ali: How did you gauge what the business was worth? Did you have a value in mind?*

*Mark:* I did. I had a value, and it was the exact number I got.

*Ali: What was that value based on?*

*Mark (putting his finger in the air and laughing):* To be honest, gut feeling. Lord Sugar always told me, 'Do you know how much a business is worth? However much someone's prepared to pay for it!'. He told me countless stories of walking into rooms and tabling offers for businesses that were totally made up. He also said that lawyers and accountants kill deals, so the rule is you'll get a feeling for what your business is worth and you follow that. Both sides have got to give a little - you've both got to lose a bit and take a bit. But as long as you want the deal done, it'll get done.

I was very lucky. I had a figure in my mind;know; I went in with a higher one, and we negotiated back into the environment that I was looking for.

*Ali: How much of that do you think was mindset?*

*Mark:* 95%. I believed I was going to sell it for that figure no matter what. And I don't know; maybe if I'd had a higher number, I could be sitting here twice as wealthy. But I knew that number was going to be fair for the business with its brand, customers, staff, revenue and the value I felt I'd put into it. We also had more five-star reviews than any other agency, tons of case studies, clients on long-term 18-month rolling contracts, and staff on long-term contracts. I had set it up as a brilliant agency that couldn't fall apart overnight. I really believed it was worth a lot of money, and I was willing to stay. There was no gun to my head. My preference was to go, but no one was forcing me either way.

*Ali: What can you share with us about the negotiations?*

*Mark:* The key to winning in a negotiation is being willing to take the deal off the table and say, 'I don't need this! If you don't want to do a deal, we don't do the deal'. Lord Sugar said to me a couple of times, 'Walk into the room, and say these words: "This is the showstopper, the deal's off!" and walk out of the room'. We used that on more than one occasion, and it worked pretty magically.

*Ali: It must have done. I think at the time deals were around 2.4x and you came out at something like 8.5x? So it was hugely different to the time. What did you do to make it so attractive to the buyer?*

*Mark:* Yes, it was somewhere around 8.5x. Every little thing culminates in one massive thing, so everything matters. I know I'm getting into some minutiae now, but this is why I'm an 8.5x man, not a 2.something man. You would get out of the lift and step into our office, which was spotless and beautiful. You would feel as though you were in Dubai and think, 'I'm in luxury. I'm in the right hands'. All the staff were in beautiful uniforms. There'd be specially chosen music playing and diffusers that always made people say, 'It smells amazing in here!'. I'd say, 'Yeah, it smells like success!'.

I was worried about all the details all the time. We would even rehearse before people came for a meeting. I'd planned when my PA would ask about coffee. We'd planned to say, 'We're not having that coffee today. Can you get the special ones?'. Every element of my business was like a play.

I know it sounds over the top, but one of my mentors used to say, 'It all matters'. I remember I went to my mentor's office for a meeting and they had a massive screen in their foyer with a picture of you on it. It would smell amazing, there would be music playing, and someone came in to meet you saying, 'Welcome, Mark Wright. We're so looking forward to having you'. It felt very cool and made you feel special. So, I implemented it in my business too.

If we had a good call online with a potential acquirer, I would invite them to the office. I wanted them to envisage themselves as the owner while they were in the foyer. So I did what I have always done. I showed them I am the owner, living a pretty brilliant life, and I don't do any of the sales any more. Come in, meet the team and have a look. It was honestly awesome, and I enjoyed selling, although it was much harder than I expected. Particularly the due diligence and legal side of things.

I'm a pretty resilient person. I think I'm probably up there, but the process tested my resilience right to the precipice. There were a couple of nights when I fell asleep while I was sitting on the sofa still working. My wife said to me, 'You've not done that since you started Climb Online'. So it was pushing me back to startup model Mark. You really have to want to get the deal done, and they really have to want to buy it because there are so many excuses for both of you not to.

But to answer your question - I just did what I always did, and I created a marketing masterpiece to sell my business.

*Ali: What can you tell me about the deal structure? I read you were very set against an earn-out.*

*Mark:* With my personality, I didn't think an earn-out was right. I'd be sitting in meetings on a long-ass handover, hearing my business go in directions I may or may not agree with, and hanging around like a bad smell. I don't think that goes down very well. I'd read a lot of books and listened to a lot of podcasts going into the deal and always heard that the money you get on the front end is generally all the money you get. So I said, 'Here's the deal, fellas. You either want it or you don't. You let me know'. A few people tried to negotiate one-year earn-outs, etc. but I was very firm on it. I was always prepared to walk away from the deal. Desperation is the stinkiest cologne. If you get desperate chasing, you'll end up selling your business for nothing because you'll sign up to a two-year earn-out where in year two you get nothing, you're out of your business, and all the shares are gone because you really wanted to sell. So, it's just making sure that it's structured in the right way to get what you deserve for your efforts.

*Ali: It makes complete sense, but I think you have to be very comfortable being able to say you won't accept an earn-out. In some deals, they question why you just want to get out, and if you're hiding something, or not confident in the business's performance. How did you get comfortable?*

*Mark:* I wasn't doing anything. I had made myself redundant. It's weird to say I wasn't doing anything. I mean, I was turning up to management meetings and things, but at that point I wasn't even the MD. I was the CEO and a 50% shareholder.

People were willing to let Lord Sugar go because he was a 50% investor and not working in the business, but they thought I would be harder to replace. So I would bring them into the meetings and show them how little I was doing. I also encouraged them to interview any of the staff they wanted and would get them to meet the MD. He was running the place and doing a fucking lot of work. I wanted them to meet the department heads and quiz them so they could see that I was doing very little and how great my team was.

They did that, and it gave them confidence that I wasn't doing much and that they could let me go. I could also show them I wasn't doing a lot because I'd invested in two other businesses, and one of the head offices was in Birmingham, so I was working there or at home. It was easy to see that Climb Online was very self-sufficient, and that I wasn't interested in hanging around to hear their hopes and dreams for the next two years. Those were their hopes and dreams, and I'd got my own vision going on.

I was very transparent about my plans with my staff and customers. I would say, 'I will make sure the new owner takes care of you. Here are the people who are interested, and here's the vision'. I introduced the purchasers to pretty much all of my employees and a couple of our biggest customers so they could interview them too. I gave them a lot of confidence that there were no smoke and mirrors. It was a proper business, and it was self-sustaining. It's all well and good being able to talk a good game, but if they get under the hood and find it's not what you displayed it to be, then no one is going to take that deal. But when they have interviewed the staff and the customers, and they're all saying the same thing - it's clear there's something tangible there.

*Ali: I love that level of transparency; it's admirable. A lot of soon-to-be exiters worry about their staff and what will happen to their team. Were you worried about that? What made you worry less?*

*Mark:* I guess it's always a concern. You don't want someone to pull down the empire you've built, fire everyone and outsource it to God knows who. You want things to be handled well and jobs to be secure. And they can give a lot of assurances, but once they're the owners, there's nothing you can do about it. You're not the owner. But they reassured us enough for us to go through with the deal, and they stood up and assured the staff both as a group and in private meetings. Once they've done that, it's on them, and it's their reputation and honour as the new owners. You can only take a person at their word.

*Ali: How did you keep the clients and staff calm and reassured?*

*Mark:* I tackled it early and held a town hall. I interviewed the key staff and clients individually before the process. I stayed for one week after the sale and interviewed them again. I asked them about their concerns and handed it all over to the buyer, telling them which people are feeling good and which clients are concerned, so that they could handle them going forward.

Some stuff was hard on my ego. Some clients were like, 'Okay, are my services staying at the same price? Ok, see you later, enjoy Australia!'. Others were quite upset. I proactively managed the process and tackled it head-on. I said, 'I'm leaving. I'm pretty knackered. I've been doing this for eight years. I'm selling to people with a great vision. The same team is going to be doing the work, and I'll still be available on my mobile. If you have any concerns, you call me personally and I'll speak to the new owners for you'.

## Reflections

*Ali: What were you most grateful for during the sales process?*

*Mark:* I had an amazing lawyer. They really helped get the deal done. Whenever I was really stressed or felt that it was over, they put my mind at ease and coached me through the process. That was invaluable. I was grateful for having an excellent lawyer, accountant, and broker. It's like anything in life - if you assemble the right team, you get the right outcome.

You also need to remember that accountants and lawyers are very risk-averse. So if their advice is that it's not looking so good, you need to be the one to say 'Let's keep going forward,' because if you listen to them too much, no businesses would ever get sold because they're avoiding risk.

*Ali: The deal is done. What happens the next day?*

*Mark:* We had 130 employees, and the company was incredibly profitable. On the day I exited, we signed up one of the biggest gaming consoles in the world, and the revenue and profit hit their biggest ever.

It was incredible. I walked through the office to leave, and it was like a dream.

I was emotionally and physically drained, which I hadn't expected. The process was longer and way harder than I thought, like some meetings at the end with the lawyers where you're going through these legal checks about what's happened over the entire history of the business. It took so long, and you're racking your brain and going through hundreds of documents. So, it was exhausting.

Also, it didn't matter how redundant I had made myself; I was always on my email, Teams or Slack checking on deals and people. Overnight, my emails went from about 500 a day to zero. I went from loads of calls to none. I had a PA and a PR person - they were gone, so I couldn't even get into my LinkedIn! I had no idea what the password was because I'd not logged into it for so many years.

So I couldn't get into anything, and everything was deathly quiet. I didn't realise how much of your identity you get from what you do for a living. If someone asked me at a dinner party what I did, I'd say, 'I'm the CEO of Climb Online and business partners with Lord Sugar'. Which sounds pretty cool. What was I supposed to say now? 'I'm an unemployed, quite rich person?'. It sounds good for about five minutes, but then what do you do?

And then I started thinking, 'Hang on. If I blow all the money, what happens then? Do I start another business? I can't do digital marketing for two years'. Plus, my phone's not ringing, I have no emails and there's only so many times I can check my phone before I'm bored.

This whole self-discovery process emerges, and while it does, it's very quiet. It sounds weird because if you said to anyone, 'I'll write you a cheque for millions. All you have to do is sign over your business', most people would bite your arm off. But you're also trading your friendships and your relationships with your customers, staff, and suppliers. It was like giving away a child. It honestly felt like a part of me had died overnight, and I'm still searching for the part of me that died in the sale.

So it's not perfect. It isn't what you think it's going to be. You will not feel how you think you're going to feel. To be successful in business, you have to love your staff and your customers, and you have to love everything about your business. If you truly love it, it'll be successful. Then when you sell, you're giving away something you love. So you can never be truly satisfied with that process.

*Ali: You had just been given the most money you'd ever had, and achieved your goal, but there was so much grief.*

*Mark:* I'm still getting over it. There were certainly 12 months of real longing for going into the office and seeing the staff, how we're looking, and having the conversations that I'd always had. I'd built eight years of my routine around going in a couple of times a week.

*Ali: And there's the pain of knowing that if you did go into the office, it wouldn't be yours any more. It would be different. The clients and staff have changed. It's not there in the same way any more.*

*Mark:* Yeah, I went there for something after I'd sold and I didn't recognise the business. It was like going back to an ex-girlfriend. It's the same exterior, but too much has changed. It was so foreign to me I never did it again. I don't know how to describe it other than to say it was empty and weird. But if I went back, I'd do it all the same. It made me a more complete businessperson, and the experience was marvellous. I've since sold two other of my companies. The experience of selling Climb Online was critical for their going through.

*Ali: Any regrets?*

*Mark:* None. I don't have any regrets; I only have learnings. I'm incredibly lucky to have had the success that I've had and the story of this sale. I often think about things I would have done differently, but you never know what the net result would have been.

I miss Climb Online a lot. And that's the best business name I've ever heard for a digital marketing agency. I love that stuff, the branding and thinking about the perception of it.

* * *

## The Future

*Ali: What would you advise an owner who wants to sell?*

*Mark:* If you want to sell your business, you have to go through the process. I would find a broker who specialises in digital marketing agencies or who has a track record. Why? They understand our lingo and phraseology. They probably also have clients or contacts on their books that they can make introductions to, and they can maximise the profitability.

You might think, 'I don't want to pay broker fees'. Those fees are a fart in the wind when you maximise the value. And they can assemble that great Avengers team around you, which is really important if you haven't been through the sales process yourself. So, I would start there and then go for the accountant and lawyer next. You might already know a great accountant or lawyer, but by choosing your broker first, you can make sure your house is in order.

They will check how much you are doing as the founder. If you're still logging into Xero, sending invoices and doing proposals, then you're 18 months from even having a conversation with a broker. You will need everything prepared, your documentation, customers and key staff on contracts, getting bad debts resolved, and customers on direct debit. These are the first questions anyone who's going to take you seriously is going to ask. If they are, 'What are your contracts?' and you say, 'Rolling contracts', they're going to just end the call immediately. I'd suggest going online and looking at questions a broker or potential purchaser might ask and answering them yourself. It will tell you quickly where you need to address before having that conversation with a broker or putting the business on the open market.

> ***Mark is (W)right. You can check your exit readiness at agencyexits.co.uk/book.***
>
> *Your results land instantly, with a roadmap that fits your stage.*
>
> *If it feels right, you can also book a call with me and the team to explore what comes next.*

*Ali: What advice would you give to someone buying an agency?*

*Mark:* Every business has got a lot of problems. It's like an iceberg. No matter what it looks like on top, there is a lot going on underneath. I've never worked at or owned a business without lots of problems. That's just the nature of business. Never get fooled into thinking that you're walking into the perfect business and you can sit back and take loads of profits and dividends. That place doesn't exist. You need to buy a business knowing you're buying lots of headaches and accept that as part of the process. You can improve it with what you bring as an entrepreneur.

You're never buying an industry or buying a product. You're buying a person or a team of people, be it the current Managing Director or infrastructure. So, make sure you're comfortable with the people at the top because that's going to be the quickest indication of whether it's going to be successful. You also have to be prepared to lose sometimes. When you walk into a casino, you don't think you're going to win 100% of the time, and buying and selling businesses is no different. Sometimes I've made a lot of money and I've made some great decisions, and sometimes I get it wrong. No matter how many deals I've done. Most great entrepreneurs still get 70% of their early-stage investment decisions wrong. That's the best guys!

So, you're probably going to make some mistakes, and that's okay. I call it kissing a lot of frogs - it's about making a lot of offers and getting yourself out there a lot. If for every 10 deals, I nail three, then they make 10 times enough money to recover from the mistakes I've made.

*Ali: What is your best piece of advice for agency owners?*

*Mark:* Whether or not you want to sell, structure your business to scale. That creates a better business overall. You do your job better, create better documentation, hire better people, and you produce a better calibre of work. It will make you as the entrepreneur do less, which is what you should be doing anyway - as much as it pains your founder ears to hear.

One day, believe it or not, you will exit your business. You will either sell it, drop dead or it will go broke. You want to sell it because that's the best of the three horsemen. You don't want to leave your business partner, children, wife, or husband with a disaster. Angling to sell usually results in a sale, which is the best outcome of any entrepreneur or business owner's setup. So, I always have that intention. That was ingrained in me long ago by every great mentor that I've ever had. It's the best advice I've ever got.

I think it makes you a better businessperson when you have started a business, bought a business, and sold a business. That creates experience - and a more well-rounded person.

*Ali: What's next for you?*

*Mark:* I've got about 17 businesses at the moment, and they vary in my share of ownership and the level of investment, but I've got some big things! Before I met with you today, I was working on another business I'm buying, and I was writing an indicative offer just as we joined. We're buying another flight school in Melbourne.

I've got a lot on my plate. I have quite a bit going on in the property scene with a property company in the UK, one in New Zealand, and one here in Australia. I have a very big flight school where we train people to be pilots. I am a pilot, and my brother is a super-duper pilot, and we're just in the middle of acquiring some other schools.

I'm always looking for good entrepreneurs and good businesses to invest in and be part of. So, if you read this book and you're looking for an investor, please reach out to me on LinkedIn, and I'd be happy to have a conversation.

I just love business and love doing deals. I love new technology and new industries and seeing what's around the corner next. I don't think I'll ever retire, no matter how much money is in my bank account. It's about being busy and doing things every day so that I feel I'm being useful.

*Ali: Is there anything else you want to add?*

*Mark:* I think the most important thing for any agency owner or business owner that's looking to sell is stuff like this book. Information is imperative. You will think that you're going through things for the first time, or that it's strange, or that it's never happened before. I promise you that pretty much every sale follows exactly the same pattern. And if you understand the pattern, you won't take it personally. You'll just understand that it's part of the process, and you'll go to the next step in the process, and you'll get a really good deal done. Knowledge is really vital for the success of the deal.

*Ali: I hope that we'll discover more of these patterns as our interviews unfold. Thank you so much, Mark. I've really enjoyed this. It's a cool moment for me because in my first agency job I was speaking at a conference in London on a small stage. I walked past one of the big stages, and you were up there! I recognised you from The Apprentice, and I remember thinking about how many people were listening to you. So it's been very cool to have your time today and to hear your story.*

*Mark:* It's my absolute pleasure, and I appreciate the invitation to be here. I think we all owe it to each other to share our experiences and help other people. That's why I do stuff like this because I was so lucky to have great mentors and great advice. And when you get there, you should help other people get there as well.

I loved every second of being here, and I can't wait to read the book. I really can't.

## Finding Mark Wright

Mark is an active investor and is always looking for new businesses and good entrepreneurs. The best way to contact him is to message him on LinkedIn.

You can find him at: linkedin.com/in/mark-wright-1658925a/

* * *

> **Want to see how exit-ready your agency is?**
> *Take the 3-minute test:* ***agencyexits.co.uk/book***
>
> **Not selling yet?**
> *Now is a great time to build for the future.*
> *Book a call and I'll show you how to scale profitably, reduce founder dependency, and build a high-value agency on your terms.*
> ***agencyexits.co.uk/contact***

* * *

## Exit Story Takeaways

**1. Build to sell from day one**

Mark and Lord Sugar were talking about an exit before they even had a letterhead. That mindset shaped every decision and meant Climb Online was always exit-ready. If you build to sell, you'll end up with a better, more scalable business whether or not you sell.

**2. Redundancy gets rewarded**

Mark pulled an 8.5x multiple in a market where 3–5x was normal. Why? Because he wasn't needed. By the time he sold, he wasn't leading sales, managing clients, or even writing proposals. If you're still in the weeds, you're capping your business's value by overvaluing your own input.

**3. Not all clients are good clients**

Early on, Mark took anything with a pulse and a budget. The churn nearly killed him. One of his biggest shifts was moving from hundreds of small clients to a smaller, more profitable agency with a stronger team. That took courage and a temporary dip in income, but it's what created long-term value.

**4. Great deals are won long before the negotiation**

From named products to five-star reviews, sharp branding to immaculate offices, Mark turned his agency into a full-blown experience. When the deal came, the value was obvious. Buyers want to walk into something that feels like it already runs at a high standard.

**5. Selling is emotional, not just financial**

Mark thought selling would feel like winning. But he also described it as grief. Exiting a business you've built is emotional, even when the money is good. That's why being prepared, both practically and mentally, matters so much. You need to know what you're walking towards, not just what you're walking away from.

# 3

# Only 4% of Agencies Sell

*"Only 4% of agencies ever sell. So, out of every hundred agency founders, only four will actually achieve an exit. The rest will either fold, fail, merge, give the business away, or be held until retirement."*
*– Luke Tobin*

**Entrepreneur:** Luke Tobin
**Exits:** 3
**Agency Exits:** 2
**Agency Exit Types:** Buy Out | Earn Out
**Exited Agencies:** Quick2Design | Digital Ethos
**Time to Exit:** 18 Months | 6 Years
**Employees at Exit:** 80
**Exit Values:** Undisclosed |Multi-Million Pound Deal
**Purchaser**: Cadastra

Luke Tobin hit the ground running. He started his first business young and had completed his first exit when he had just turned twenty-one.

Inspired by this, he has gone on to found and exit a succession of businesses, including two marketing agencies. The second of these led him to an unconfirmed, approximately £8 million exit (*leicestermercury.co.uk*).

Perhaps what makes this even more of an achievement is that Digital Ethos was set up in Luke's 'spare' time around a contract role. He took just 6 years to reach his multi-million pound exit and was only working full time in the business for 4 of those. It also led to Luke's 2 years as Co-CEO EMEA of his approximately $50 million revenue buyer, the Brazilian leviathan, Cadastra. Having started many businesses, Luke was catapulted onto the group's board, leading a team of 860+ with 9 offices, over 400 clients and operations in multiple countries (*Cadastra*) whilst becoming a successful investor with a powerful and diverse portfolio.

I was so excited to sit down with Luke and hear what he has learned from his multiple exits, investing, and deep understanding of starting a business from zero and creating something that has true value. With his commercial and practical insights, he certainly did not disappoint.

* * *

## The Entrepreneur

## Origins

*Ali: How did your career begin?*

*Luke:* Well, like many others reading this book, I often feel like the agency life chose me rather than the other way round! I wanted to be an actor when I was younger, so I went to drama school. I jumped around a lot on stage in my younger years and got a scholarship to an acting university, but decided to defer it. So I ended up scratching around for a year or two doing direct sales jobs, which I absolutely loved. I was able to use my drama skills to develop my raw confidence to go out and start selling different packages. I began by selling experience day packages and also did charity fundraising. There were all sorts of random jobs for me early on, but it gave me an excellent initial start in that sales minded world.

After that, I decided to do a stint in recruitment and did three years for my sins! Not many people last a year in recruitment, let alone three. It was a good grounding, and it meant I could hone my outreach and lead generation skills.

I've always been entrepreneurial, with a business as my focus, or at least one on the side. In my early twenties, I ran a wine and spirits import company that sourced products from overseas and sold them to festivals and events. I loved it; it was a fantastic opportunity to gain experience in understanding the various components that make a business tick. It was one of those archetypal "360" roles where I had to wear many hats and develop empathy for the different parties, understanding their pain points and how I could best "grease the wheels" to ensure a great experience for everyone involved.

Those varied jobs broadened my skill set and ignited my desire to be at the centre of it all, the one pulling the strings, so to speak. So I jumped back into the world of experience days, but this time I decided to do it for myself. I set up an e-commerce store and started selling different packages, from car racing days to hot air balloons. Then I went to Australia and did the same there. I leveraged direct sales teams to ensure our sales funnel wasn't one-dimensional. I had 40 or 50 backpackers in Australia selling different experience day packages at shopping centres and on the high streets, basically at any high footfall location we could find. I later launched the same business model in the UK and later sold that business.

It's through that experience with the e-commerce company, I realised the importance of understanding marketing, particularly digital marketing. So, I'd been upskilling myself as much as was possible back then. Google was still pretty new, and they'd just acquired what was then 'double click', which became 'AdWords', and the whole Google takeover of everything digital happened. It was a fascinating time to be in this emerging space. I realised that everything was on the cusp of change, and I wanted to be at the forefront of it. I decided that if I wanted to immerse myself in this world, I'd need to sharpen my tools and learn from those who were leading the charge, so I began working at a Google Partner, selling some unique IP that really excited me. I knew it was the start of something, but I could never have foreseen where those decisions would've taken me at the time.

*Ali: It's so interesting that a lot of the successfully exited founders I speak to started out in sales. It's no surprise that when it comes to packaging their company to sell, all of those skills help them win those deals.*

*Luke:* Yes, sales is fundamental. It's one of those things where new revenue fixes most problems. And if you're the founder who can go out and get that revenue, you don't have to rely on other people to do it. That puts you in a really strong position for sure.

*Ali: How old were you when you exited that first business?*

*Luke:* I had the business when I was 18 or 19, and I sold it when I had just turned 21. So it was early on, but it was a small exit. It's nice to reflect on, and someone paid me some money for it, so it is an exit, but as life's gone on and my experience has grown, my perspective has shifted, and there are obviously varying exit levels. The exits that hit the press are very different from those five and six-figure ones when I was younger.

Each time I have exited, it's gotten bigger and better, which is part of the journey, I guess. But that's not to downplay the importance of those smaller businesses and the role they played in shaping me. The fact that someone was willing to sign a cheque to purchase something that was all conjured up from a figment of my imagination was somewhat of a spiritual awakening for me. And in that sense, nothing's changed; the pride and sense of ownership you have when you take a vision, convince others to join you in pursuing that vision, and ultimately hand it over when it doesn't need you as its life source... Well, I think in that, we've probably stumbled on my purpose for being here.

*Ali: How did you come to start an agency?*

*Luke:* As mentioned previously, I began working for that Google Partner, and I was there for about 3 or 4 years. Whilst there, I set up Quick2Design because the company I worked for did pay-per-click only and needed landing pages to convert leads successfully. When I asked them, "Where do we get landing pages?" They were like, 'Oh, you can use third parties.' And I thought, 'Okay, well, why don't I just be the third party?'. So I set that up and started serving all the other sales guys and people in the business. There were 80 of them, and most were using my services for landing pages, which was great! It was during that period that I honed my skills and understood how an agency worked. I really hated the no-man's-land that sat between client expectations and the agency itself; there was always this weird element of mistrust and misalignment. So, I tried to bridge that. Eventually, I sold Quick2Design to a similar business that basically wanted to bring it in-house.

It was a rapid 18-24-month cycle to then sell it. It wasn't a large exit, but it was great to see how quickly an exit could be achieved if solving a very niche problem, and if I'm really honest, I didn't want to be running a web design company longer term. It was good overall, but it's just not my passion.

Following that, I did a contracting stint for a German software company. It was a lot of fun, and I was travelling and doing about 30-40 flights a year. I got to see a lot of the world. I did that for the best part of four years. I also started Digital Ethos alongside that. Because it was a contract role, I didn't have any restrictions, and I ended up growing Digital Ethos to 14 people before I then went full time.

*Ali: What skills do you have that made you right for leading a successful agency?*

*Luke:* Having had those earlier exits and small wins along the way has helped, but also my failures and missed opportunities helped to build resilience. I'd also had a very varied career background, touching on four or five different industries and selling to 50 or so different types of businesses.

As a person, I've always been innately entrepreneurial and curious, and had an innate desire to understand how and why things work. I can walk down the high street where I am now in Portugal, and I'll look at a restaurant or a business, and I'll be trying to figure out how well it's doing and how it works. I've always had this curious nature to understand how a business operates and makes money; that's definitely helped me.

In regard to this more recent exit, I started that business with the ambition to sell at some point. Some of the work I do now involves supporting people in scaling their businesses to sell. It's about, 'How I can make this thing sellable?' and start that as early as possible. For example, how do we de-risk it for a buyer now, even though you might not want to sell for three or four years? Because if you get those principles and hygiene points in place, you're going to have much more of a chance of success later on. The stats are pretty scary. Only 3% of businesses sell, and only 4% of agencies do. So, out of every hundred agency founders, only four will actually achieve an exit. The rest will either fold, fail, merge, give the business away or be held until retirement. It's kind of crazy.

*Ali: What are you most proud of in your career?*

*Luke:* There are a few things. I'm certainly proud of my own growth that's happened in that time. Coming at things from a sales point of view, and even the drama background, creates an element of outward confidence that's sometimes a bit forced. What I've realised over time is that I have grown into being a good leader as well. Initially, I was a bad manager because I was too focused on my own KPIs and goals. Early on, you're still trying to prove to yourself and to everybody else that you have some value to offer the working world.

Having that journey of discovery has been really good. Now I am finding I have a lot more purpose, and I'm able to support other founders and entrepreneurs, which I can see makes a huge difference and helps them to shape their success. I find a lot of day-to-day joy in that.

*Ali: Do you regret anything?*

*Luke:* Oh, millions of things. I try not to look back too much in anger, right? There's no point in regret. It's all part of the stepping stones. In hindsight, it's really easy to say, 'Oh, I probably would have done that a bit differently. Maybe I would have gone faster?'. When we were growing Digital Ethos, I had 14 staff before I went full time. Because I'd had some mixed success early on and I'd had a couple of failed businesses, I was always trying to be one foot in, one foot out, to protect myself and my lifestyle and income whilst testing the water. Digital Ethos had already shown me in those first couple of years that it could scale, but I still wasn't quite committed.

I wish I'd gone all in because by the time I went full time in January 2019; it was a year before the pandemic hit and all that craziness. We still grew exponentially. At one point, we were the fastest-growing UK marketing agency, achieving 80% year-on-year growth over five years, which was amazing. So I probably should have gone harder and gone all in sooner. I really believe that to make something a success, you need to put momentum behind it, and the only way to do that is to make it your full focus.

*Ali: It's a tricky balance, isn't it? It's natural to want to mitigate risk. Most people don't want to get too deep into something and find that they've lost everything, or they've made a big decision that's catapulted everything into chaos. How do you try to find that balance? Is it a gut feeling?*

*Luke:* It has to be partly gut feel. As humans, we often try to ignore our gut feelings, but if we trusted them more, we would avoid many pitfalls. As you establish yourself professionally and build a strong leadership team, you can gain a sense check and some grounding from the input of those other individuals. Over time, I've become much better at hearing those voices, and a lot of that comes down to hiring the right people and trusting them. Getting better people around you than yourself means you can leverage those skill sets as well. I think acting on your gut-feel is absolutely critical.

## Mindset

*Ali: I'm curious, what is your mindset when you're evaluating risk, or how to grow a business?*

*Luke:* Mindset is probably 60-70% of the battle, especially as an entrepreneur, right? You are going to come up against so many pitfalls, so many challenges, and so many times when you think, 'This is probably not even worth it.' You have to stay clear on your vision. So, having a strong mind is essential, and there are many ways to reinforce that mindset. You can build that from healthy habits like sleep, exercise, meditation, and constant education, as well as all the things we see all over the internet. It's probably overdone a little these days, but you can indeed build a resilient mind. But it's also about having a really clear, laser-sighted vision of where you want to get to and then pulling yourself back out of the weeds every now and again.

*Ali: I often help agency leaders who have a big goal, say it's exiting, a revenue target, or a profit figure. Often they'll have what is happening day-to-day, and then they have this big goal; and the two are disconnected. They're talking about the vision, but there's no clear path to get there. How did you get around this problem at Digital Ethos?*

*Luke:* It's taking that vision and then getting people to implement it through change management and day-to-day support structures. It's challenging to be honest. As a visionary and a founder, it's probably the hardest thing to deal with, as you need to instil that vision in other people. And that's why having a good leadership team and finding people who want to come on that journey with you makes this a lot simpler. I reinforce this through constant feedback loops and regular goals for each individual, all aligned with the core objective, which is absolutely critical. Typically, in my businesses, we always have short, mid, and long-term objectives that are tied back to being able to hit that overall objective. So, everybody's accountable. They all feed back regularly in one-to-ones, and we make sure that we stay aligned that way.

* * *

## Building The Agency

### Development

### *Ali: Tell us about Digital Ethos.*

*Luke:* In the early days, I was testing the water. So I had another contract job that was 30-40 hours a week, and I was travelling a lot. When I was away, I could be anywhere - Finland, the US, or wherever. I'd have to attend one or two meetings, and then I'd have a lot of space and time to wait for the next meeting. I found it really productive to spend that time testing the waters. I remember building the website for £100. It was a landing page, and I just got out my mobile and started calling previous clients. I was also buying leads from some websites and testing. So I was selling to anyone that would have me and then figuring out the price point and whatnot..

I quickly realised that I couldn't deliver it all on my own. So I started getting some freelance support, and in the end, I had maybe 20 different freelancers and about 30-40k a month in revenue, and I was like, 'My God, it's too much to manage now. I need at least someone full-time to help manage these clients.' I was fortunate that people weren't churning, which surprised me, given that, looking back, we had a weird

ICP (ideal client profile) of loads of different sectors and all relatively small businesses. The service level cannot have been that good. I think they just liked having me, and I was fairly knowledgeable. Sometimes I would forget a report for a week or two, or be chasing a freelancer who was behind, and somehow the clients didn't churn. God knows how in hindsight. Then we started bringing in team members, and obviously, we got a much better kind of cadence for the clients. Over time, we developed a much more defined ICP, and we specialised more, but it was sporadic at best to begin with.

*Ali: What were your core services? I read that SEO was your bread and butter.*

*Luke:* It was. We adapted over time. It's interesting because the previous agency I worked for only sold PPC, but initially, we weren't doing much PPC with Digital Ethos. It's kind of perverse when I think about it, but we were doing a lot of SEO, and the reason that I leaned into SEO is that when I looked at the marketing stack, SEO was in high demand, and it was very easy to pitch a 12-month+ retainer. What I liked about that was the stickiness. So all businesses that I build now are sticky revenue-wise. I love retainer businesses.

Many agencies that rely heavily on project work often experience significant fluctuations and struggle with new business. So I wanted something that was sustained and where I could see clear growth.

When we brought in other services that were more demand-led, people expected results much quicker, and so you get more elements of churn.

After SEO, we bolted on PPC; we had that natural angle of 'whilst you're waiting for SEO to perform, you have PPC'. Then we touched on social media, but to be honest, I've always struggled with social performance organically. But now, ironically, through my personal brand, I've spent time learning how to make organic social work; and I now get it more than ever. But for a long time, I felt like it was a 'nothing service' and that a few posts on social media were not going to do anything. But now I understand it fully. It just wasn't my background.

Then we brought in PR, web design, creative, and became very much 'full service', but we did it gradually over time. I think SEO specialisation actually really helped us early on because we were pitching SEO for the first 12-18 months as a single service. We were going in with three packages and asking people which of the three they wanted. Quite often we were signing people there and then, which was great.

*Ali: So the journey was from a narrow service offering with a broad ICP, to a broader service with a narrower ICP?*

*Luke:* Yeah, we found that having a broad focus of clients initially helped us identify our sweet spots. We had a split of 50% e-commerce and high-growth brands and 50% really boring B2B businesses. We had two separate teams to deliver them. The B2B clients were great and the stickiest, and the e-commerce clients were very demanding. The e-commerce was the sexy stuff the staff wanted to work on, and then we had the more boring cash flow machine. It was quite a nice way to split it, but I remember trying to explain that to my buyer and they said, 'Yeah but they're so different?' and I explained, 'Yeah it is quite different, but there's also a deliberate hedge in that; and it kind of works because of it.'

One thing we never did was specialise in one industry specifically, such as becoming an e-commerce only agency. We stayed relatively generalist, which, if you read a lot of the books, they will tell you is not the right thing to do, but it worked for us.

*Ali: I love this debate. I often get asked by founders whether they should just focus on law firms or food, or whatever it is. The way I worked with my sales team was very much more generalist. We had a target, but we also had a spread, which gave us stability. You only have to look at the pandemic to see that if you were specialising in hospitality right then, it would have been a really difficult time. As you say, the books don't say that. They say, 'Pick one, get your vertical, get your industry, narrow it down'.*

*Luke:* As a founder, you have to be willing to focus on new revenue at all costs until you can be confident in your ability to service or niche. And there should always be a bit of a spread.

At the agency I sold into, they had three or four core ICPs and were very particular about sticking to them. I understood why because they had proven it over 25 years and built loads of case studies. If they went into a pitch with those case studies and with that background, they had a 75% chance of winning that pitch; even against the big network agencies. So I understood why that had made sense. But for us on that smaller scale, I knew we needed to test and iterate.

I've fallen into the investment world now, entirely by accident, like all things in my life, it seems! In investment, the principle of diversification is considered the key to long-term success. Certainly, I found that in the agency world. We had times when certain industries were hot and others were bust, and by having that diversification, we survived and kept thriving throughout all of it.

There were a lot of times we brought new salespeople in, or even new directors, who had ideas about specialising. I didn't feel comfortable doing it, given my experience with different market changes. So look, it worked for us. Not everything works for everybody the same way, but staying somewhat generalist was a bit of a superpower for us in the end.

*Ali: The flip side of this is that not all clients are the right clients. So there's a balance where everything has to be able to be delivered well operationally, and we have to be sure that we're not selling so broadly as to create a wild churn machine that needs constant feeding, like a hungry beast.*

*Luke:* It's about people, isn't it? I would say that for every ten clients we brought on, we had one monster. Clients are amazing, but sometimes people can present so nicely in those early stages. And then, my God, they can run you ragged within weeks of bringing them on.

One thing I became very good at was parting ways with clients. Initially, it goes against every fibre in your body, especially if you come from a survivalist background. To begin with, I was apprehensive about doing it, but I did it in the end. For us, it was about ensuring alignment, especially with the team members whom I felt a duty to protect. The immediate example that comes to mind is when I decided to terminate the relationship with our second largest client. It had gotten to the point where the relationship had become so toxic that members of my team were on the verge of mental breakdowns from having to appease their insatiable demands. Seeing individuals in tears following certain phone calls was the line in the sand for me. Sometimes, as a leader, these are the decisions that need to be made. They hurt at the time, but bold decisions made in the best interest of your team pay back 1000X in the long-term.

So in summary, we could've theoretically grown quicker, but growth brings its own problems, so you have to take a holistic view and not be blinded by the money signs.

*Ali: I'm a fan of having flexible criteria so that in times where you know the going's good, you can be that bit more rigorous about who you do and don't want. When things are lean, then perhaps you flex that a little more. So perhaps you would have grown 200%, but it's all the gremlins that get in the cupboard when you do that, isn't it? They're in there throwing out staff who are unhappy, messing up processes, forcing refunds or making late payments, and it chips away at that growth percentage anyway, doesn't it?*

*Luke:* Definitely, it does. For every good, there'll be a negative consequence somewhere, and I think in agencies it's usually the team that suffers. So if you bring in that amount of growth, you're probably not hiring quickly enough to fulfil that level of work.

## Growth

*Ali: What did your growth look like?*

*Luke:* It's probably one of the key differentiators of how I built the agency compared to most other agencies I know. It still surprises me that when you look at the agency landscape, around 93% of agencies don't have a full-time salesperson, which baffles me. It's normally because they come at it from a discipline background where they've been really great at something. That's not to take anything away from them. They weren't necessarily business or entrepreneurial people, or they know they're very good at a discipline. They've fallen into this structure where they've had a few referrals and they've managed to grow a reasonable agency to 10 people off the back of their knowledge, experience, and clients. But then they hit this wall and realise that they need to actually go out and find new clients if they want to keep growing. Well, that's a whole new skill set.

I came at it completely the other way round. I loved marketing, and I understood marketing, but I wasn't really a marketeer. As a businessman and salesman, I identified a niche and opportunity in the growth of marketing services, which I saw as a chance to capitalise on. I wish I'd done it a bit earlier as well, because I think I could have made it a lot bigger. Even so, I was coming at it from a different angle.

By the time I sold Digital Ethos, we had seven full-time salespeople. At the beginning of the cycle, it was just me, and within the first three or four months (bearing in mind I was not full time), we had another salesperson. By the end of year two, we had three, and then we just kept on growing the sales team. So, we were, for want of a better word, 'aggressive' with our sales. But don't get me wrong, we were retaining clients as well; which is the key because you don't want a leaky bucket.

So we were trying to do both elements of that see-saw that I spoke about. You've got to keep the sales going, but if you're not careful, stuff starts falling out at the operational end. So we had to find that balance.

To be honest, I look back on those early days now and I feel for the team. They were working extremely hard to keep pace with the amount of sales that were being brought in. At one point, it was around 7-9 clients a month, and it was amazing; however, servicing that level of growth to a high degree of customer satisfaction was a new learning curve we had to embark on.

*Ali: It sounds like you had that first salesperson in really fast. Was that with an exit in mind or just purely growth perspective?*

*Luke:* In the first couple of years, it was just me and a bunch of freelancers, and I was doing all the sales. We started hiring in early 2018, with around 15 people onboard, and I realised I needed another salesperson. I totally understand that you're never going to find somebody who pitches in the same way as the founder, but that's okay as well. You just need people who can facilitate those meetings. I always think it's essential to stay in that sales cycle for as long as possible as a founder. It's very easy when you find someone else to do it to go, 'I'll pull myself out of this now,' but I stayed as close as I could for as long as I could. So stay close to it, but invest in the sales engine early.

*Ali: My background is that I put the first sales team in for an agency, so the founder could step away. The process worked well, and we doubled the agency. But there were a lot of challenges along the way as ever.*

*Founders often ask, 'When is the right time to put someone into sales?'. It's a major lever in how the business functions and performs, and it's very difficult to let go of. When do you think is the right time and how would you approach it?*

*Luke:* I'll start by saying there will often be nuance in decisions like these. Many elements will influence the time and the manner in which the sales engine changes in its function. In my case, it made sense to bring people in to focus on lead generation and nurturing. It meant I could focus on other areas of the business, and I could focus on larger, more strategic deals.

As I've said many times before, new revenue solves most problems, so it's essential for all owners to never turn their back on the sales process entirely. Hire the right people, define their rules of engagement and make yourself available to support them both operationally and to help them get the larger deals over the line.

* * *

# The Exit

## Preparation

*Ali: Did you always think you would exit one day?*

*Luke:* Let's be honest; in a service-based business, there are so many variables that you can try to think are in your control, but often you need a sprinkle of luck, timing, and a few things on your side. I always had the ambition to sell. I had a bit of a rough roadmap, but then I was knocked off course a few times. I launched in Germany and Canada in late 2021. Canada was okay; Germany flopped. I thought, 'Oh my God, what have I done?'. I bought an agency and made two acquisitions that year as well. One of them failed. So, there were all of these setbacks along the way. At those times, I was thinking, 'This is a nightmare. How am I ever going to explain this to a buyer?'.

It's good to have a rough roadmap. I can wholeheartedly say that now every business I start, I am building to sell from day one. I already have an idea of who my target is, and I've got a persona that I want to start courting from day one. I'm doing all the proper hygiene, building data rooms, and trying to de-risk the business in every way that I can.

*Ali: So, as you plan your business, you're not only planning your ICP for those you're going to sell the actual service or product to, but also for those you'll sell the business to?*

*Luke:* Absolutely. When I'm evaluating whether it's a good business, I'm doing both of those things alongside each other. And if I can't see a clear person to buy it, there's no point in building it because I'll be stuck with it.

Don't get me wrong, I will build great businesses, but I don't want to operate them forever. That's what I've learned. It's the gift of exits and having some success that have made me realise that I don't want to operate businesses for the long term. There's always an element of operations that needs to be done, and managing people, but for the most part, they are there to support other operators rather than me being the core operator.

*Ali: You've built start-ups and you've worked for gigantic businesses (like*

*Co-CEO at Cadastra). What do you prefer?*

*Luke:* I'm definitely a 'zero-to-one' guy. I've realised I'm probably not the best person to handle the day-to-day bureaucracy and running of the company when it reaches a certain size. I sold Digital Ethos to a large international organisation and was a Co-CEO there, focused on EMEA. It was a great experience, but that kind of corporate piece isn't really for me. Some people thrive on it, but I prefer to be a bit scrappier and solve problems at the ground floor level, where I can actually make a difference. I don't mind putting a shirt on, but I'd argue I do my best work in a T-shirt.

*Ali: When is the right time to exit?*

*Luke:* Selling a business when the founder feels they've given all they can and they've reached their limit is actually a really good thing. So ideally you're still on the up. But often they stay there a bit too long and burn out, or they just feel exhausted, and that energy ripples through the leadership team and trickles its way down to the other team members. And actually, a lot of agencies that have experienced significant growth reach a certain size, and the founder gradually takes on more responsibilities. It's like the opening scene in the *(Ali: Spoilers!) Top Gun* sequel, *Maverick,* where he's just pushing the plane that bit harder than he should, and everything shakes - and in the end it crashes.

It comes back to what you were saying earlier about the founder knowing what they want and alignment. There's absolutely nothing wrong with an agency founder reaching a point and thinking, 'I'm happy here.' If that's what you want, if it's a lifestyle, then that's alright as well. Not everyone needs to try to take over the world.

As part of this other business I am building, I've interviewed 50-60 agency or creative service businesses, and not one of them has said they didn't want to exit. All of them want to exit at some point, even if they're lifestyle businesses, and they want to sell it somehow. So everyone needs to think about 'What's my number? What's my limit?'. And then reverse engineer that to decide what their decision point will be. However, you need to establish the principles along the way that will enable you to reach that outcome.

*Ali: Absolutely. I think there's also a question here about tolerance. For example, if you're a lifestyle business, it's working out what you are willing to tolerate to get to the point of sale, and whether that is what you actually want. It could be that you're torturing yourself with a goal when you don't actually want to do the things that are required to get there.*

*Luke:* Yes, and my God; it's hard work, isn't it? Let's be honest. Building an agency is probably one of the hardest ways to make money. Service-based businesses are driven by people, and people you can't control. You can guide them, you can nurture, you can support, you can incentivise - but you cannot control. So you are literally at the demands of your client's ebbs and flows, but also your team's abilities.

There's always an affordability piece where you have to consider how much you can afford from a team and skill set perspective. Building an agency is a tough way to make money, and understanding your limits is key to avoiding constant burnout. I did burn out. I definitely did. I found many moments in that last journey where I felt trapped. I had to just work through those burnout stages somehow and come out the other side. I definitely pushed my limits, that's for sure. The one thing that made all the difference in the end was surrounding myself with great advisors, people who had walked the walk. This, in my opinion, is something that all founders should invest in.

*Ali: I think an agency will do that to a person. They are chaos and have a reputation for it. But my goodness, being the person who carries all that weight is a tough place to be with so many people relying on you.*

*Luke:* Yeah, absolutely.

## Negotiation

*Ali: I read you got several offers in 2022. I think they were unsolicited. Is this what led you to think it was the right time for you?*

*Luke:* Yes, they were unsolicited; however, I'd specifically structured the business with an intention to sell, so, by design, we were naturally attractive to the M&A market. I think the positive press we had around buying agencies and opening in Toronto and Hamburg made a lot of noise and brought eyes to the business. We also won a few awards that year, a Drum award and a few others. We had four or five M&A consultants reach out asking if I would be interested in selling.

And at that point in the back of my mind, I always knew I was interested. But I'd actually just started thinking about setting up a group, doing more acquisitions and trying to scale. So, I point-blank rejected the first couple without really hearing them out.

Then one opportunity that came along was from a large private publishing company. I won't say who they are, but they are in Germany and they're the second largest in the world. They reached out and said they would love to get into digital marketing. They'd noticed that we had a Hamburg office, and their head office is in Hamburg. They asked if I would like to go over and see them. I actually ended up meeting in Amsterdam, and we had a three-day workshop together.

I was talking about the industry, the cycle, while they shared their vision for a product they planned to launch and how we could contribute to it. It was slightly different from our ICP, and there were elements of uncertainty in some of their plans. So, I was open and honest about my perspective. So they tweaked some of the model, and actually, that deal looked very interesting. It was arguably bigger than the deal I took in the end. However, a few factors related to the Ukrainian war and other issues caused that buyer to panic. It was good that it happened because I'd already had a couple of excellent conversations with Cadastra to whom I sold the business.

*Ali: Tell us about the deal.*

*Luke:* I really like the gents behind the business. There are three founders, and they are very entrepreneurial by nature. They are Brazilian and very warm. I found a lot of alignment, great energy, and good vibes from the meetings I'd had with them. So, coming away from that other deal and then leaning into this opportunity was a great decision. We got to a great place. It also gave me a position on the board, and the chance to step into a larger corporation, which was something that I hadn't experienced before at that level. So, I was definitely excited about that.

*Ali: What an amazing opportunity to step into that co-CEO role!*

*Luke:* Yeah, it was great - 800+ staff across 9 global offices. The core language was Portuguese. The whole thing was fascinating and an authentic experience. I was there for about two and a half years in the end, and I'm pleased with the decision.

Digital Ethos, as a brand quickly disappeared to become a unified business within the larger global entity. So Digital Ethos has been dead and buried for quite a while, but it's now part of this much larger global infrastructure. It felt like a natural home and also a progression.

*Ali: I don't think you used a broker?*

*Luke:* No, they did on their side.

*Ali: Okay, so their broker reached out to you. What can you share about the negotiation process?*

*Luke:* I had a couple of business advisors. Every business founder or entrepreneur should have a coach who facilitates some of their gaps. So, I had a couple. I had one on the finance side because it's an area that I've become better at over time, but I always wanted that sense and sensibility around that. And I had a commercial coach as well. So we got together and thrashed it out. I felt the first four or five offers I received were all 'lowball'. Whether that was on a multiple of EBITDA or however they priced it. I think most of mine were around 3-5x, and in the end it was much closer to 7x.

So you just have to try to move the needle and negotiate. It took almost six months to broker a final position, and at one point, I was on the verge of walking away before making the final decision to proceed. You have to stay true to your idea, and you need to be realistic about what the market will pay. Like anything, it's only ever going to be worth what someone's willing to pay, but at the same time, you have to make sure that you're comfortable.

In a negotiation of any type, each party needs to feel slightly uncomfortable at some point, and then you find a middle ground. And that's certainly where I got to in the end. That was the right thing for both parties. But it's not for the faint-hearted. If you're going to exit your agency, you have to put on a different lens and realise that it is just a commercial business decision and not be too sensitive about it.

*Ali: It's such a tricky point. You've got your baby, and you're handing it over.*

*Every scrap of the business has come out of your brain, or your team's, and it's been made with care. So, it's difficult to separate the personal feeling about what the value is of all that effort and the amount of life and sleepless nights you've put into building it.*

*Luke:* Definitely.

*Ali: How did you separate those things?*

*Luke:* With difficulty; patience and time are the key. The beauty of the negotiation piece is that most of it is done in written form. It's for various reasons, from legal to just practicality, but also to remove some of that emotion.

You have to make a lot of courting calls and attend meetings, but usually the offers come in written form. So you get a bit of time to process, get some support, grab a few cups of coffee, and then you can go back. I think that's important.

It's getting past that initial period. Normally, you have some heads of terms, and then you move into a restricted period of 30, 60, or 90 days where you can't talk to anybody else. In that time, the due diligence process starts. That's actually the time when it feels the most personal because that's all your dirty laundry up in the air, and everything starts to get exposed. There are a lot of questions about everything that you've done, how you've operated, and why you made certain decisions. You need to keep a balanced view of it and put yourself in their position. All the buyer is trying to do is de-risk that environment, as you would as well.

*Ali: Can you tell us a little more about the structure of the deal?*

*Luke:* So mine was slightly different, and this is public information. I sold a certain amount for cash up front, and then the rest was traded into stock. So, I became part of the group structure. It was the right decision for me. I wanted alignment with what the business was doing. There was always this ability to come out of the business after two or three years, and that was always part of the plan. So, really, my objective as co-CEO was to integrate Digital Ethos into the larger entity, ensure everyone was comfortable and happy working together, and then to step out of the leadership role.

*Ali: There's some interesting debate about earn-outs because a lot of the information out there says that the money you get upfront is all you're going to get. Whether that's right or wrong, I think very much depends on the deal.*

*Luke:* It does.

*Ali: Would you do an earn-out again if that was on the table?*

*Luke:* I would definitely structure my deal slightly differently next time. Maximising as much upfront capital as you can is critical. So is making sure you have really clearly defined milestones for how you're going to be paid that money and why.

Tying everything only to future growth is challenging. There should be other metrics in there too. Things like staff retention and senior leadership team growth play a big part. Team integrations also offer significant long-term value to the business, but they aren't always compensated for. Usually, the focus is just on the growth number, and using that as a crude metric can be pretty difficult. For a lot of the agencies I speak to, those numbers can be very high - sometimes even higher than their historic growth. So is it realistic?

When you're negotiating, you need to make sure the goals you're setting are realistic for you to go after. You could have a baseline and a top line, with an accelerator clause in there. For example, on the baseline, let's deliver what we've always delivered. You're buying the business today at this value based on continuing that trajectory, so keep things similar for the next couple of years and pay me out - that seems fair. If we go up by 10–20%, then you trigger the acceleration clause.

But a lot of buyers come in and say, 'This is the acceleration clause you need to hit to get your payout.' And if you can't hit those numbers, you're effectively giving away half the business. So, you just have to be very careful.

Overall, I was comfortable with my deal. There are definitely things I would have negotiated in hindsight, but that's just part of the journey of life.

*Ali: How did you handle the news with your team?*

*Luke:* I only told my senior leadership team that I was in these negotiations. The rest of the team, whether because of maturity or experience, may not all have taken it well. After the deal was signed, I gave a presentation, and to my surprise, everyone was actually excited. And I was really pleased that everybody stayed for at least the next 6 months. There were a few people then who left naturally, but certainly not because of the sale. I was really proud of that, and I wanted to make sure that was the case.

I wanted to make sure everyone's jobs were secure. If you sell to another entity, there's always an element of re-evaluation - even of your own role in the long term. It would be naïve not to think that, but I was pleased that everybody retained their jobs and were in a good position.

You need a few people around you that you can be honest and open with, because otherwise it will eat you up. That's why those coaches or third-party mentors are invaluable. If you don't have them, consider one or two senior team members you trust. I would have them sign a statement or a non-disclosure agreement (NDA) that restricts their actions. It gives that extra level of protection so that even if they're friends with a couple of people in the team, they will not start slipping after a couple of glasses of wine because that could quickly destroy the business before you've even sold it.

*Ali: The team's safety and wellbeing is often a big fear for the owner before an exit. What other fears did you have going into it?*

*Luke:* There was a lot of uncertainty and worry about meeting the criteria of due diligence. This happens even though you know you've run a great business. You have this element of 'Oh God, but what if?!'. Especially when they drill down into the specifics of things such as churn levels and the reason each client left over the last two years. It's just part of the process, and actually knowing that now makes it much easier. I would say to people, just go with it. The buyer probably knows most of the reasons anyway. The main thing for me is I wanted to do an excellent job for the team, but also for the new buyers as well.

I've always been proud of being able to deliver well in whatever I do. And I wanted to make sure that there was cultural alignment, opportunity, growth, and also for yourself, there's always this fear of 'What if I'm not needed anymore?', 'What happens when this is over and I leave eventually or my earn-out finishes?', 'What does this look like for me?'.

So I think there are a lot of different elements that give you fear and sleepless nights, but in the long term, you have to remind yourself that work doesn't define us. It obviously helps give us a sense of purpose, but once you achieve a successful outcome, you can move on to the next thing. I think every founder goes through it, and there's also an element of founder's remorse that happens after the sale as well. That last exit I had, we signed the paperwork late on a Friday, so the money didn't hit until Monday, and I was sitting at home on my own working a typical day. So the money hit my account, and it was very underwhelming because there was no one around to celebrate with. It felt like, 'Oh, okay, this is weird. It's no longer my agency. What happened? I'm still managing the team, and I haven't told anyone yet.'

Many founders find that month or two really hard; they have this seller's remorse and start thinking, 'What have I done?'. Once you come through that, though, and you get clarity, I think it's always a good decision in the long run.

## Reflections

*Ali: There's definitely an enormous sense of grief for some owners. Do you think with Digital Ethos that was mitigated or shaped differently because you had the opportunity to go into the Co-CEO role?*

*Luke:* That definitely helped. Absolutely. And I was excited! I took three weeks off for a lovely holiday, and then I went straight to Brazil. I literally landed back in the UK from the Maldives on a Saturday, and on the Monday, I flew to Brazil to spend time with the leadership team. There was a real air of excitement and energy in everything we were doing. That really helped with that piece. I have to say I didn't have seller's remorse per se. I had a few moments of thinking, 'Oh, you know what, I could have done that on my own, blah blah blah'. I think that's normal. But I felt really energised and happy to go on this next step. It had taken me the best part of 12 months to complete the deal, so I'd gone through a lot of those emotions before even actually completing it. I think having a clearly defined role of what you're going to do post-sale is important.

*Ali: What's your advice for anyone planning an exit?*

*Luke:* The best time to start planning that exit is today. In terms of how to go about that, we need to look at this from two different perspectives: operationally and strategically.

The first angle is an operational one. Try to look at your business objectively. Consider the information a buyer would look for and almost request that from yourself. You can easily go online or ask ChatGPT for a due diligence list. Go through it, and see what it looks like. *(Ali: Or head to agencyexits.co.uk/book and take the exit-readiness test for yourself).* The main aim here is to view your business through the lens of the buyer. Consider how to de-risk; this approach will not only facilitate a smoother transaction but also safeguard your valuation and the final outcome. Get your house in order; ensure you have a data room built with all relevant documents, data and information. Ensure you have a defined org chart with succession planning for all key personnel. Standardise and professionalise your internal assets - ensure all processes are documented; methodologies are defined and detailed; and most importantly, prepare your financials! Your buyer will want to understand your pipeline, your conversion rates, your top sellers, your current churn, and your likely churn. Don't allow room for any surprises later down the line.

The second angle is strategic. The one thing you'll never be prepared for is the sheer emotional and physical burden an exit process can place upon you. Typically, a sale can take anywhere from 3 to 12 months to complete. During this time, remember that you still have a business to run, along with all the associated challenges. The absolute best advice I can give is to surround yourself with trusted experts. I cannot emphasise this enough; without the trusted advisors I placed around me, there is simply no way I could have kept the sale, the business and my own mental health above water. You'll need advice on the obvious, like legal and finance, from people who understand your sector. However, the most important support that you'll need, which is sometimes the most frequently neglected, is advice from a founder who has been through the process before. As I alluded to earlier, the emotional fatigue that comes with a sale process is enough to take the most seasoned founder to their breaking point. This individual will act as an anchor in the process to help you stay focused on the end goal.

*Ali: What's the biggest mistake an agency can make on their exit journey?*

*Luke:* Wait until they're burnt out and desperate and then try to sell. I think that's the majority, actually. They get to a point where they're thinking, 'Oh my God, I just want to sell this thing now.' That's the worst time to sell. The best time to sell is when you actually don't need to and you're in a position of power. As in any negotiation, you don't want to go in and be on the lower ground. Unfortunately, statistically speaking, about nine out of ten businesses are sold in an element of distress, whether that's founder distress or the business's. And that's just not good for anyone.

*Ali: What is your recommendation for someone who wants to acquire an agency?*

*Luke:* If you've got a good agency already and you want to bolt on additional services, that's an obvious place to look. Go and find somebody who's already done it well and look at whether there's some alignment in culture and then bring them in. There's also an argument for 'like for like' if there is a similar client base or similar specialities. That's often a nice merger. I think the best way to do that is by getting into those circles of other agencies and trying to understand the founders, what makes them work, and trying to do some alignment.

For me, I always look for opportunistic deals as well. So I was looking at the other side, knowing that nine out of ten deals are done in distress. I would look at the for sale websites for agencies and see the listings that were not using a broker. Sometimes I'd reach out, and a lot of times they were in distress, but they might have a good business there. So, look at those as opportunities as well. Just bear in mind that if you buy those businesses, you're going to have to take on whatever that distressed element is behind the scenes. So if it's just the founder, that's fine. Remove the founder. But if that's filtered through to the team, you've got to deal with the situation, and you've got to nurture the individuals involved and bring them back around. So there are loads of ways to cut that, but always look for value ad or cultural alignment.

* * *

## The Future

*Ali: How do you see AI transforming the future of agencies?*

*Luke:* Oh, huge question. Massive question. Many smaller agencies will probably struggle to survive unless they pivot quickly. Much of my current work focuses on providing solutions for this issue, and helping businesses integrate more agentic principles and automation is essential.

I was at an AI event in Paris a couple of weeks ago, listening to the VP of Google. She mentioned that two years ago, Google utilised 10% AI in its marketing campaigns. This year, it's 66%. By next year, she thinks it'll be nearly 90%. She doesn't think their thousand-strong marketing team will decrease in size, but it will also never grow. As Google grows and continues, she doesn't feel like it will ever need more people. They are just retraining those people to be more agentic-focused. Someone asked whether she saw the changes as an agency killer in the long term. She said absolutely not. They've been at the core of agency journeys for years. But those agencies that used to have 100 people and had to grow to 200 to serve additional clients will probably be able to stay at 100 people because one person who is trained agentically can deliver so much more than they ever could before. So, there's this revolution that needs to happen.

The problem is that many team members are reluctant because they feel their jobs are on the line. The argument actually is that if they don't adapt, someone else will be brought in who can lead and work with agentic software or systems. So, they need to pivot fast. Agencies of 10 people can now do what agencies of 100 used to do, but most agency owners are not ready for this change. So, I actually think there will be a huge cull at the bottom end. The larger network agencies, such as Omnicom & Publicis, are investing billions into their own LLMs (large language models) and building their own solutions around this. They're not doing that by mistake or by accident. They're doing it because they know that's how the market's going to go. So if you are a smaller operator right now, and you aren't pivoting, you need to pivot fast.

There'll always be a world for agencies in different shapes and forms. I believe that combining human experience with agentic outputs is beneficial for the industry in the long term. It means that if you have a great creative who designs something bespoke and draws something beautiful, and then puts that into AI, the AI can spin out 50 ad variations. That's efficient. It means the client's not overpaying for something that would have taken too long before, and it means you can actually deliver faster, arguably maybe more quality, but if you're not ready for that pivot and other agencies are, you'll be killed off.

*Ali: What's next for you?*

*Luke:* Well, as I'm sure others who've exited have said, there's always the question of 'what next'. For me, the sale transformed my life. But after any seismic change, you're often left questioning your purpose.

In that period of reflection, it became clear I wanted to help other founders break through the glass ceiling of an industry that often demands a pound of flesh in return. At Unusual Group, I've built the framework and team to help them do just that. We provide best-in-class back office, mentorship, guidance and strategy - and, if needed, access to capital to accelerate growth.

We deliver this uniformly, with a strong peer-to-peer support structure. I'm enjoying being able to support founders in all the ways that, from experience, would have helped me in my own pursuit of the '4% club'. Built by founders, for founders, Unusual Group provides the support and infrastructure needed for our partners to scale and sell.

## Finding Luke Tobin

You can find Luke on his website luketobin.com or on LinkedIn at: linkedin.com/in/luketobin/ To explore Unusual Group further, head to unusualgroup.com

* * *

> **The best time to plan your exit was yesterday. The next best time is today.**
>
> *Take the 3-minute Exit Readiness Assessment and see how close*

> *you are to building a sellable, founder-independent agency. Your results and action plan land instantly.*
>
> ***agencyexits.co.uk/book***

* * *

## Exit Story Takeaways

**1. Start with the end in mind**

While most of us start out by thinking about our target client, Luke takes this a step further. He builds every business with a target buyer for the agency already in mind. It's important to think about who your buyer might be and what they would need to see to make your agency a safe purchase.

**2. Sales drives everything**

Luke scaled Digital Ethos more easily because he put salespeople in early. He stayed close to the sales process but didn't leave the agency's revenue depending on him. This is an enormous step towards reducing risk for a potential buyer, because they can see how the agency will survive without you.

**3. Exit before you're exhausted**

The worst time to sell is when you're burnt out and desperate. Buyers smell distress. Luke stresses that the best deals happen when you don't *need* to exit, because that's when you have negotiating power.

**4. Plan for due diligence today**

Buyers will pull apart your numbers, your client churn, and your processes. Luke advises building your data room early and not waiting until you're already in talks. That way, you control the narrative and reduce risk.

**5. Structure the deal to protect yourself**

Earn-outs aren't always bad, but they can be brutal if the milestones aren't realistic. Luke recommends maximising upfront payment and ensuring any future targets are achievable and clearly defined.

# II

# Lead Machines

# 4

# Cobbler's Shoes

Bill Nash's science brochure company spent years trying to make a brochure for itself. In the meantime, client brochures were designed, printed, distributed, and redesigned. Generations of client brochures passed, and Bill's company still had none for itself. Frustrated with his team, Bill called his direct competitor and asked if they would make their brochure for them. The second brochure company exclaimed that they had exactly the same problem, and so they ended up doing each other's brochures because it was the only way that they would ever get done.

It's a story that my client and friend, Nigel Wilkinson, talks about when I mention cobbler's shoes and agencies. Fortunately, Nigel is a patient man, because having loved it the first time he shared it with me, I've asked him to wheel it out in front of several audiences - including an agency dinner in front of a bunch of other founders, and now for you too.

Suffice it to say that as a marketing agency owner, you know a lot about marketing. Yet when I first meet agencies, often lead generation will be in the top three problems that they would like to solve. It's not that they don't have all the knowledge they need to do it; it's that they have too much. The roller-coaster effect is the main saboteur. You may recognise it. It's the one where leads are looking low, so you resolve to put some time into your own marketing, then the client work lands and so it's all hands on deck! As the work completes, or a client churns, leads look low again, and so up and down it goes.

In the next two interviews, we'll meet Tim Cameron-Kitchen and Andrew Bloch - masters of creating marketing agency lead machines that would allow them to complete their agencies. They approached it in very different ways, with Tim being very performance marketing focused, and Andrew's approach being fuelled by PR and brand.

I share them with you because to exit for a great valuation; you have to make yourself redundant. The most difficult piece of this is often that you are the main new business winner. Leads come to you because of your network, but if we remove you, the conveyor belt stops.

# 5

# Cultivated Discomfort

*"I've learned that there is a value to just hanging in there when it seems bleak."*
*— Tim Cameron-Kitchen*

**Entrepreneur:** Tim Cameron-Kitchen
**Agency:** Exposure Ninja
**Employees:** 80+
**Exit Type:** Still the owner, CEO in place

Building a sales team from scratch is no mean feat. There are moving parts *everywhere*, and unless you turn 'chaos' into 'process' pretty quickly, you find yourself scrambling to personally close every deal in the pipeline.

That's exactly where Tim Cameron-Kitchen was. Brilliant at winning business personally, but without a scalable system to take himself out of the salesroom. That changed when I joined as head of sales. Within a year, we had a proper team up and running, with systems in place that kept the whole operation running smoothly. From qualifying leads to restructuring discovery calls, reshaping proposals, and setting the rules of engagement with clients, we built a process that brought in *the right* type of business: the kind of clients who would stick around, and not churn straight out.

By that point, Tim was already well out of the sales trenches. And the business didn't stall. Far from it. Over the next few years, as I moved into broader commercial roles, we doubled the size of the agency from around 30 people to over 80. Exposure Ninja became less dependent on Tim and more of a platform that could fuel his acquisition ambitions.

For Tim, it wasn't about building a simple business to coast on, or preparing for a big sale. In reality, he *never* wanted to sell. His instinct is the opposite: the moment things feel comfortable, he shakes them up. He actively seeks new discomforts – whether that's acquisitions, side ventures, or stretching the agency into fresh territory – because each challenge keeps him sharp and pushes him on to the next level. For some founders, the goal is completion rather than exit.

That's the thing about cultivated discomfort. You don't chase 'easy'. You don't avoid the hard stuff. You lean into it, again and again, until discomfort becomes the very thing that drives growth.

Here's how Tim tells it.

* * *

## The Entrepreneur

## Origins

*Ali: How did your career begin?*

*Tim:* I was a drummer when I came out of my music degree in 2007, and I wanted to be a musician. I needed to make some money because I didn't want to teach music like everyone else. So, I set my drums up in a studio, well, a 'studio' is a very generous term for it - I set my drums up in someone's back garden and I recorded for people over the internet. I wanted to make money doing this. So, I had to build a website promoting my services. That's when I learned how to build websites in Photoshop and the basics of SEO and Google Ads. So that got me addicted to marketing. Fast forward a few years to 2011, and I built a website for my next-door neighbour, who was a plasterer. That did very well for him. I ended up building an agency on the back of that experience.

*Ali: A lot of founders I speak to say they fell into it. Do you think that's fair to say of you too?*

*Tim:* 100%. I really enjoyed my drumming, but making a career out of it just sucked all the joy out of it. I realised that the thing I most enjoyed about the drumming was impacting someone's songs - the music that I was recording was mainly garbage, so I didn't really impact it. When I built that website for my neighbour, he kindly said it completely changed his life. I thought, 'Wow, my significance score has shot up through the roof,' - which is one of my primary drivers. I thought, 'Forget the drumming, let's build some more websites!'. The process from there was pretty organic. I built websites for other trades like plumbers, electricians, roofers, scaffolders, and gas engineers.

Then, in 2011, I wrote a book called *How to Get to the Top of* Google, which was about the process that we were using to rank these websites. I'd already built out a small team. The book took off and drove a lot of leads. I chose the name Exposure Ninja for the agency after being invited to talk on someone's webinar and needing a name immediately. Then, step by step, me and my team built the agency from there. It was never the plan. It was never a career aspiration. It just sort of happened, really.

*Ali: What skills do you have that made you right for leading agencies?*

*Tim:* I honestly have no idea. I think being hard-working and just caring a lot. I think if you care, then you find out how to do the things that you don't know how to do. I honestly don't know where my skills lie. I've become reasonable at making videos. I've become reasonable at a few different things, but I'm not sure that any of them were *the* skill that I needed to build an agency. I think it's a case of just caring more, being willing to put the work in.

Another thing is acting on feedback from clients. If I look back at Exposure Ninja, every improvement that we've made has come from a complaint or a client having an issue. Then it's about taking those issues and finding where they came from to fix the core part. I think that's quite a useful thing, but I wouldn't necessarily say it's a skill of 'mine' as such.

*Ali: You're being so humble. Others have said, 'Oh, I'm great at sales.'*

*Tim:* But they're amazing at sales because they have to be, right? Often the trap for agency founders is that they become amazing at sales, and that becomes their crutch. It becomes their entire identity, and they become so engrossed that it shapes their personal narrative. 'I'm the person who goes out and hunts and finds the clients and brings them to the agency so that my team can feast and I look back with pride'. You know, that's awesome. But that skill set isn't always there from the start. That skill comes from, 'Well, shit, someone's got to sell some stuff, otherwise we're never going to grow!'. They obviously know a lot about the thing that they're selling because they built it or they were doing it to begin with. So, it ends up that they're quite good at sales. I think what I found with Exposure Ninja, and you actually helped teach me this, is that although I thought I was quite good at sales at the start, it turns out I wasn't the best salesperson at all.

If I'd have clung on to, 'I need to be good at sales', that would have really held the agency back. Sometimes accepting that you're not great at any particular thing is a useful way of putting the team in place who can run the company autonomously because you're not clinging on to this aspect as your identity.

*Ali: I guess that is probably one of your superpowers. You're very good at getting deeply interested in a particular area that needs fixing. You learn it, figure it out, run all around it and draw the map, and then you figure out how to give it to someone else and hope that they can do it even better. I think that's an important skill for leaders, particularly within an agency where things move so fast you have had to do everything as the founder.*

*Tim:* Yeah, that's really interesting and a useful skill in business. Since Exposure Ninja, I've bought a couple of renewable energy businesses. One of them I'm fully in at the moment. My original goal was, 'I will not be on the org chart. It's going to run itself'. All of that stuff. It's probably six months away from running itself. But in order to get to that, I've had to get so in depth rebuilding the sales team, building out the sales process, and getting really into the detail. I think it's one of those where you have to do it because if you care about the survival and the growth of your business, you put the work in. You spend that time doing it. You know, when everyone else is chilling out on a Friday night, what am I doing? I'm doing leg day and then smashing out another three hours of building out a sales proposal because I care enough to do it. I don't know whether it's a skill or whether it's just an absolute, relentless determination not to stop until it's fixed. But either way, that thing is definitely important if you want to build an agency that they can either sell or step back from.

## Mindset

*Ali: Mindset comes into building a good agency, but also being able to complete one. What has been your mindset throughout your journey to completing your agency?*

*Tim:* I think recently I've learned that there is a value to just hanging in there when it seems bleak. I can't tell you the number of times I've thought about quitting or selling or giving up over the years and have just never done it. If there's a challenge, there's a value to hanging in there. I'm thinking about when you watched Andy Murray when he used to play tennis and there'd be these games where you think, 'This guy is fucked – he's out, he's just totally done for,' but he's just hanging in by a thread and if you just hang in there long enough, eventually you can grind out a bit of traction. Then you get some momentum, and before you know it, you're back on top, and you're winning!

There are different ways of quitting too. I've spoken to agencies from an acquisition perspective, and a lot of times people think of selling when their agency is at the bottom of a dip, and really they're selling from a place of desperation because they just can't face the fight anymore. Whether it's that they've had a terrible year, or they've lost a bunch of clients – often it's the market giving them some feedback and letting them know that the thing they're selling is no longer relevant and they need to pivot.

It's important to have the energy to get through that, and to answer the tough questions that you're shying away from. Stop telling yourself, 'Yeah, but people are always going to pay for a human experience or people will always pay for X'. That's clinging on to an outdated mindset that they actually need to let go of if they're going to get to the next level. So, I think that aspect of mindset is really important.

*Ali: What are you most proud of across your career so far?*

*Tim:* It might just be how I'm feeling at the moment, but I don't really feel that proud of anything that I've done. It's one of those things where the further you work your way along, the more you realise there is so much more to do. I don't need to feel comfortable. I don't need to feel proud. I want to feel uncomfortable. I want to feel like the lowest performer in the room. I want to surround myself with people who are just on a completely different level and calibrate myself to that. So, I look at what I've done, and the Exposure Ninja team is unbelievable - they all do things I could never do. The agency is doing better than ever since I stepped away from it. So, I could feel proud of what we've done there, I guess. But really that's the team's achievement, do you know what I mean? I just don't feel like anything I've done is worthy of pride.

I need to feel like I'm fighting some battle. I don't need to feel like I'm at the top of any mountain. Might just be how I'm feeling today.

*Ali: Knowing you as I do, I think of you as a 'What's next?!', not a 'Look at where we've got to,' kind of guy.*

*Tim:* Yes, absolutely. It's a kind of cultivated discomfort.

*Ali: Do you have any regrets?*

*Tim:* I regret not pushing harder to go bigger. Since getting into the renewables stuff, I've realised that I've never worked hard before. There were times at the start of Exposure Ninja where I thought I was working hard. Looking back now, I was not working hard. I thought I was stressed, particularly during COVID. I was not stressed. There are other levels above that of stress. And I'm sure there are levels way above where I am now. But what that's taught me is that my capacity for hard work and stress is way bigger than I ever imagined. And if I'd known that 10 years ago, my God, I would have pushed this thing so much harder.

I don't know whether that's a legit regret because I think Exposure Ninja is a nice place to work. We have amazing team retention. The team is very happy. It's a very loving and, I guess, comfortable environment, which I wouldn't change for the world. That's the DNA of Exposure Ninja. It's a very safe place, and the people are very happy. It's a stable business with consistent profitability and regular recurring monthly revenue, and all of this stuff, which is amazing. But it makes you wonder, could I have pushed this thing 10x if I'd have really driven it hard?

* * *

## Building The Agency

## Development

*Ali: I know this story so well I could tell it myself, but we should hear it in your words. Tell us a bit about Exposure Ninja, including how it started and how it evolved over time.*

*Tim:* It began with the book. It started generating a lot of inbound leads, which is a thread that's run through Exposure Ninja. We've always had a lot of inbound leads because we've always been good at getting attention, whether it's from books, YouTube, podcasts, or Google. The agency formed around the lead flow that we were getting.

We were getting known for SEO and content marketing, and then we noticed that the websites that we were working with were rubbish. So we had to build websites, and then we added pay-per-click, conversion rate optimisation, and email marketing. We added different departments for each of the follow-on services, with the overall thread coming from our very early work with the tradesman. If you're selling a tradesman marketing, you better generate some leads this week or you're cancelled. You have to kill your supper if you're selling to really small businesses like that. And I think that legacy continued throughout Exposure Ninja's journey. We've always focused on trying to make as much money for our clients as possible, knowing that if we can do that, they'll continue to pay us and we'll continue to grow.

That was the evolution of Exposure Ninja. I started as the founder and then gradually started building a team. We built a reasonable sized team fairly quickly. We actually overbuilt to about 100 people at a crazy low revenue per head. I'd always taken the approach that we need to systemise. So we'd built this large detailed infrastructure which over the last few years we've, I wouldn't say dialled back from, but we've focused on recruiting and keeping high-quality people that can take a bit more of their independence and can think a bit more outside the box. Today we're a team of about 75 across all the different areas.

We've got a specific sales team, marketing team, dedicated senior leadership team - all the infrastructure of a much larger company, but obviously at a much smaller revenue.

Of course you know that because you built out the sales team, which has been crucial to our growth.

*Ali: I have worked with so many agencies since Exposure Ninja that I can see* some things that *make it unusual. I think there are three: 1) that it's fully remote and has been since before it was cool, 2) the enormous amount of inbound leads that come to the agency, and 3) there is a relentless focus on performance and results.*

*Tim:* I think that all three things came from our very early days. In my drumming era, I was fully remote. I was the first fully remote grass roots unnamed session drummer. I had to build that industry myself because I hated going to the studio and wasting half a day in travel when I could just smash out more tracks remotely, and so Exposure Ninja was always built that way. Our first hire was in the Philippines, and we built out a Filipino team and many of whom are still with us today. It was always part of our DNA, and that comes from an efficiency perspective as much as anything. We also realised that being fully remote meant we could hire the best person for the role even if they lived somewhere other than in a three-mile radius from our office - which is probably not the optimal selection criteria if you're trying to find the best people.

On the inbound leads piece, for me, marketing and direct response marketing is the highest calling of man. Nothing beats the feeling of generating leads and seeing business growth. That's my love language, right? It's inbound leads. It's seeing businesses grow. Whether it's ours or a client, nothing gives you that sense of significance. Going back to Ben the plasterer, why did it change his life? Because of the inbound leads, right? You can't get any better than that. So, we always marketed Exposure Ninja because it matters. If you're a marketing agency and you're not marketing yourself, just think about that.

The results-driven focus goes back to the tradespeople days. Everything is about how many leads we can generate for these businesses because otherwise we're going to get cancelled.

## Growth

*Ali: What did your growth look like?*

*Tim:* When we first started, new business looked like more inbound leads than we could handle from the books. The books did really well early on, and there was always a good volume. It was volume at the start. It was volume when you were with us. It's still volume. With volume, there's not a huge amount of filtering. If you get a book on Amazon and it's a bestseller in the digital marketing category, you get all sorts. You get everyone from someone who is starting a hemp bracelet company and wants free SEO, to the global marketing lead of a FTSE 500. You just don't know what you're going to get.

So, in the beginning, it was volume with no filtering. Then it's been trying to systematise the process as much as possible. I remember the only unprofitable month we had at Exposure Ninja was in October 2014. We'd actually gone against the remote thing, and I'd set up an office in Nottingham - against my better judgment, and it really didn't work. We filled it with local people. We built a sales team of people who didn't know what they were doing, and, unsurprisingly, our sales tanked. I had to make a very tough decision and let half of the company go.

I think there were nine people at that point. I let them all go on the same day. I did half of them on Skype because they were remote. I fired the entire office. I stood there, told them, and cried. Then they gave *me* a hug. And I remember thinking, 'Oh my gosh, I'm so visibly broken that the people I've just let go have come and hugged me'.

Anyway, the next day we had to sell more stuff because we still had people in the agency. So, I signed up for a CRM and started building out a systemised sales process with automatic follow-ups. The goal of that was to manage this inbound lead flow by myself. So I had to figure out a systemised way of doing it with as much automation as possible.

That was the early incarnation of sales, and I was just doing it myself. The automated system worked really well. November 2014 was the best month that we'd had until then; December was the best month after that. And I was like, 'Great, this is working!'. Over time, it became clear I couldn't manage the leads and actually couldn't run the business because I was always doing the new business. There was a period of about three years of hiring salespeople that didn't work. I tried hiring young people, hiring experienced people, hiring on commission only, hiring people on salaries - and it was really difficult. I couldn't figureout what was going wrong, but it was going wrong. So I hired all these people. They'd sell a bit here and there. But our sales were 95% me, and then the others would bring in dribs and drabs, which would then have problems on the accounts later.

That all changed when I met Wayne. He understood things, and we were similar in a lot of ways, so he could fit into the process. He didn't need whatever was missing with the others. He had it, and it worked. That was a real relief because now there were two of us. Then we met you when you were our client, and I remember saying to Chris, who was your boss, 'Ali is a rocket; if you ever get fed up with her, I'll take her in a heartbeat'. I think I mentioned that idea to you too. To my joy, that ended up happening.

*Ali: Yes, I called you and said, 'Hey Tim, I need to make a change and I want to work at Exposure Ninja. Can we do something?'. And you said,*

*'I'll see what I can do'. I remember checking my phone when I was in a kickboxing class and you'd messaged me saying that you'd cobbled together a half-account-management, half-sales role to get me in.*

*It was a wild ride. That only lasted 6 months before you put me in as the first Project Management Team Leader, and then 6 months after that I was your first Head of Sales. We grew fast.*

*Tim:* Yes, I'd had a walk to the gym one day and thought we've got enough leads that I could hire people. If I hired three people who were half as good as me, we'd be net positive, right? And I thought, well, they're definitely going to be half as good as me. I hired them and felt like we had a sack full of cats that would need herding. You were so competent. So, I thought let's get Ali to run it!

That was a really great decision because you understood the agency, how to build systemised scalable processes, you had been a client, and you understood our sales. So you could organise it and take it to the next level, which was transformational, and it's been a continuation of that ever since.

*Ali: A lot of the agencies I speak to don't have the luxury of lead flow. It's often referrals, and usually they're having trouble finding the time to do their own marketing. It's often a bit 'boom and bust' where they realise leads are low, do some marketing, stop marketing to service the work, and then panic again in a few months.*

*Exposure Ninja's lead volume of several hundred a month is unusual. I think people might be interested in how it does that.*

*Tim:* I've always taken the position that we need to have a lot of leads and that the way to get them is by educating people. So, this started in the drumming days because I love direct response marketing. I love lead generation. I'd be running these ads in drumming magazines teaching people how to do online session drumming, which is my thing.

Most people are running a half-page ad in a magazine and generating a bit; often, they don't even know how much because there's no call to action (CTA). Well, I'd have a hardcore CTA. This ad looked so ugly. It was intentional. The design team would be like, 'Please, mate, can we tidy this up?' and I'd say, 'No, just run it like that because I know it's going to work'. In the trades business, I'd do the same thing. I'd get an article printed in a magazine like 'Plumbing and Heating Monthly' talking about how to generate leads through your website. I'd know when this article went live because at the bottom of the article it was like, 'Text this number for a free DVD', and my phone would be red hot for a day because the magazines hit the people's doorsteps. They're all texting, and I can't use my phone because the leads are going off the whole time. With Exposure Ninja, I wanted to do the same.

The tradespeople knew nothing about digital marketing. So, I wrote a book that told them how to do this digital marketing stuff. And it wasn't ego-y. It was literally showing them the process that they should follow. I knew people would read that and think, 'I can't be fucked with that,' and would request a free website and marketing review from Exposure Ninja. So, all the businesses have had some sort of CTA, a compelling next step, and an education-focused information marketing angle, which then drives people to the CTA. It's how I've built everything. It's how the renewables business is going to be built. It's how we're going to triple this thing in about a year. Exactly the same process because that really works. It blows my mind that marketing agencies aren't marketing themselves effectively. With the educational pieces we'd put out, leads would come through and they'd say, 'I just got to say, guys, I absolutely love this whole thing that you're putting me through'. If we can't do that, what the hell are we selling you? If we can't be good at this thing, which is core to what we're delivering, what else matters? So for me, if you've got that, you can build a business. If you don't have that, business is a real struggle.

*Ali: A cornerstone of Exposure Ninja's wildly good inbound leads is the book that you wrote. How did you get it done?*

*Tim:* It wasn't the first book that I'd written. I'd written a book for the drumming business because I saw a video from someone that said writing a book is good for credibility. And it's just a 30,000 to 60,000-word document. So I didn't overthink it. I started with the goal and what I needed to teach people. I broke that down into sections, and then the sections into chapters, and started writing.

The first version of the Google book took two weeks. I remember sitting on my bed writing it, just cracking it out. It was absolute rubbish. Full of spelling mistakes, full of grammar mistakes. I didn't even read it. I designed the cover myself. It was an absolute dog. It didn't do anything at all. Then I got a cover designed, and that did a lot better.

People would love the book, but they hated the number of mistakes in it. So they'd send me these long emails with things like, 'On page two you've got this, on page three you've got this'. And would send me all of these changes. I've got to be honest; sometimes, I didn't even make the changes because I'm a starter, not a finisher. So I just would be like, 'Yeah, cool. Sweet. We'll fix that in the next edition or whatever'.

It started doing really well on Amazon, and it became a bestseller, and there were a few things that helped that. We'd run a free promo where we'd make it free so that loads of people would download it and then we'd switch off the free promo. Back then, I think that your position on the bestseller list was the number of purchases or downloads over a 24-hour period or something. So, you'd switch off the free promo and it would go to the paid list, but it would stay at the top of the paid list. So, you'd be at the top of the bestseller list. And if you could do that and the book was good, you'd maintain that position. So, that's what we did. And it was a consistent bestseller for years. It wasn't that competitive then. We'd be selling more books than, like, the Dragon's Den biographies.

Now it's so much more competitive. The book still generates us some leads, but it doesn't generate us anywhere near the volume that it used to. It also generates smaller leads than the leads that we're going for now. We basically take all the revenue that the book makes and the audiobook and put it into ads inside Amazon to keep it selling because we're using it as a lead generation and credibility piece. We're not using it as a moneymaker. So, my advice about the book is probably don't bother.

*(Ali: Oops)*

* * *

# The Completion

## Preparation

*Ali: When did you decide to step back from the agency and why?*

*Tim:* I don't know that I wanted to step away from it as much as I'd had a bit of an existential crisis over the past few years. We grew quickly, and then it was relatively flat for a few years, and I'm energised by growth and newness and chaos - and it didn't have that. It had stability and calmness, which most people love. But for me, it was boring, or it didn't feel like it needed me as much. If there was a crisis - great, let's do it! Let's dig in! But in the calm world, it didn't really help. So, I wondered what's wrong with me. I had an executive coach to work out what type of CEO I wanted to be. And the more I did all this research, the more I felt that being a CEO is not for me. It isn't a job that I would apply for, and if I did apply for it, I wouldn't even get an interview. And if I got an interview, I definitely wouldn't get a second one. It's just not me. I'm a starter, I'm a fixer. Once it was stable, it just didn't feel like me.

So, I said to the leadership team, 'Guys, I don't think I should be CEO.' And they said, 'No, no, it's absolutely fine. You figure out all the things that you want to do because no two CEOs are the same, and we'll fill in the gaps'. So, we did that for a year or so. And it got to the point where I thought Exposure Ninja was essentially operating without a CEO because I was just doing the marketing, doing videos and playing with the AI tools. You don't need a CEO in that role. I felt it would be so much better if it had a dedicated CEO. So I started talking to Charlie, who was our COO and started in 2014, and I just threw it to her and said, 'What do you think?'. She was happy to do it and it turned out to be a very good thing. It allowed me to play with other stuff and create chaos elsewhere. And it was an amazing thing for the agency because guess what? Our business is better when it has a proper CEO. We've grown since then; our margins are better, and everything's stable.

So, I guess it came from recognising that I'm not a great CEO and actually didn't enjoy it anyway.

*Ali: So, a big part of completing your agency is having the right team in place. How did you go about it?*

*Tim:* Recognising the things that I wasn't good at and making sure that we had people that were great at those things. And it also meant that I wasn't always going to agree with how those people approached things. I wasn't looking for a team of yes-people. Charlie, our COO, who then became CEO, is a great example of this. We wouldn't agree on everything, but she's organised. She's clear-headed. She takes things away and thinks about them. She has great ideas, but she doesn't have on-the-spot ideas that just fire off all the time. She's not an idea hosepipe. She's a thinker, and she's very considerate. I thought that was exactly what I didn't have; she needed to be on the team. And then it's just about finding people who can fill all the gaps until you've got a complete team.

I think one of the biggest mistakes we can make is to think, 'In order to replace me, I need to find someone who just looks exactly like me. I'm just looking for an identical puzzle piece that can just slot in behind me' - but they don't exist. They're horrendously dysfunctional, and they're probably a founder somewhere else. So, that's not the approach to take at all. Instead, find someone who complements you and then build in the other skills around that. That's been the approach I've taken.

*Ali: What is the most common thing you find the founder is still doing that they absolutely shouldn't be?*

*Tim:* Sales. I ask acquisition targets, 'What's your sales process? What's your new business process?'. And I know the answer before they even open their mouth is, 'My personal network, people that I've spoken to, leads come to me'. And then you say, 'Okay, so what do you want to do?' and it's often, 'Well, I want to go. I want to go travelling. I want to move to New Zealand'. So then we have a conversation about what happens if we take them out. What will new business look like? Well, there is none, right? Complete disaster. So, the founder needs to build that new business machine before they're ready to think about an exit. Otherwise, the only other solution is you're going to get peanuts for this thing because there's nothing to buy.

*Ali: So, many people who are reading this are still in the thick of it. How do they get from being heavily reliant on them to an agency that's completed and now they have options? They could sell it. They could stay in it. They could do whatever they want with it, but it's no longer solely reliant on them. What would your advice be to them to help them get there?*

*Tim:* I think knowing what the organisation chart needs to look like is quite important. One mistake I've noticed when I'm talking to founders who are trying to exit is that they find a number two and then the number two's role is so muddy and weird because the number two is just taking on everything that the number one doesn't. That's not an organisation chart - that's just complete founder dependency but with someone else in the mix to be reliant on. We started by trying to make as much money as we could so that we could afford to hire at each level of management. We started with department managers. So I didn't need to worry about any of the delivery. Once we had department managers, we then had a general manager who could take care of those. And then it was the sales and marketing piece and putting in a head of sales and someone who is dedicated to the agency's own marketing.

So, then you're gradually easing your way out by putting people in underneath you as the business can afford to and prioritising the stuff that you know you're not good at and that you will not spend that time on. Don't give away the thing that you spend all of your time on and you're really good at. Save that until the end. Make sure everything else is taken out first because if you're really good at it and it's what you spend all your time on, it's going to take you so much time to get rid of that. For most people, that's sales. So you don't want to also be running the entire company and trying to find a head of sales. You want to have the rest of it done first, and then it gives you a bit of time and flexibility to get the sales piece right so you can hand that over, and then you're free.

*Ali: Yes, it's really common for the sales piece to be the last one. It's hard to let go of because the agency can't survive without it. There's a genuine struggle because often the founder has been doing it since day one, and they've accumulated so much information and so many tactics over the years that they have trouble downloading that information into another person. It's part of what I loved about building the sales team, and what I enjoy working with agencies now. There's a whole journey of codifying that information so someone else can pick it up and run with it.*

*Tim:* Yes. One of the other mistakes, and I'm sure I made this mistake myself, is holding on to the good leads because you know you can close them. You need to give them to someone else. If you have the luxury of leads, it's much easier to do that. I had to rationalise with myself that if I'm 100% of the agency's sales, I can replace myself with three people closing 50% of the time, and we'll have grown 50%. And if they can all be half as good as me, that's fine. As long as we've got the lead flow, happy days.

Otherwise, it's really difficult to hand those over, and you're always going to be looking over someone's shoulder and micromanaging. You're always going to justify to yourself why you should be involved, and why you should be the hero. Whereas actually, you just got to say, 'Right, fuck it, whatever happens happens, go and do it'. And they'll mess up the first ones. Their conversion rate will be low at the start, but if they're good, they're switched on, and you give them the support that they need, they'll get better. Within a few months they'll be destroying you anyway because they're spending all their time doing sales, and you were never spending all your time doing sales. And guess what? It turns out you weren't that great at sales, anyway.

*Ali: Yes, one of the biggest mistakes I see here is not giving team members sales training. I like to put in* systems, *like using bingo cards to get all the information in discovery calls, and frameworks. Otherwise, stuff gets missed, and then everyone is surprised that it doesn't work out.*

## Acquisitions

*Ali: What do you look for when you're acquiring a business?*

*Tim:* I spoke to 200 agencies when I was looking to buy an agency. The main problem with most agencies is the founder wants to exit to do something else, but it doesn't take you long to figure out that the founder is the tent pole. If you remove them, the tent falls down, and there's no value there at all. It's a complete washout. We found this time and time again.

You either find a founder that wants to stay in and they're happy and they want to work with you and grow it, which is fantastic, and you could do that, or you find a self-sufficient machine that the founder actually can step out of. But as an acquirer, what I don't want to do is go into an agency where the most valuable employee, who does 90% of the sales and 20% of everything else, if not more, then leaves. The business either collapses immediately, or I've got to try to replace the founder myself or find someone else who can. So, I think the biggest thing is founder dependency. Any buyer is going to look at that as a massive risk.

Even if you say that you want to stay on, as an acquirer you are giving this person a huge amount of money. Are they going to be motivated to close sales? Are they going to be motivated to go on a sales call at 7 a.m. on a Saturday morning because they're talking to an overseas client? No, they're not because I've just paid them a life-changing amount of money. So, I'm not going to do that deal. I think that makes most agencies unsellable, from my experience.

*Ali: What are your thoughts about working with a broker?*

*Tim:* An agency I almost bought fell apart because the broker had coached the agency owner to the point where there were lots of things that weren't true. So the broker must have said, 'In order to maximise value, you need to say this, this, this, and this'. During due diligence, and I'd spent £20,000 on due diligence at this point, it turned out that those things weren't true, but the broker had told them to say it, so it fell apart. In my experience, and I've only got experience of the big brokers, the main value that they add is listing the business for sale. The difficulty is they want to get themselves inserted between the buyer and the seller so that they can justify their fee. That makes it incredibly difficult as a buyer because I just want to talk to the seller, and I want a personal relationship with them. I want to ask questions and get honest answers. Otherwise, I don't know what I'm buying.

When you're going through a broker, everything's muddier. They're trying to position things. They're trying to angle it in the right way. There's a reason such a small percentage of broker-listed businesses sell. Now, having said that, if you're not using a broker, it can be quite difficult to find a buyer. The great thing about the brokers is they often have extensive networks, so they can fill up your diary with appointments straight away, which I think is a value add. I'm just not sure that they add much to the sales process itself. So, I think it's something that sellers have to think really carefully about and weigh up. Don't just default to, 'I need to find a broker to sell my business'. You've got to make sure that broker is actually adding value and actually wants the sale to happen.

*Ali: Who do you need on your side to get the deal done if it's not the broker?*

*Tim:* You need someone who is very good with numbers. I've tried to buy a couple of businesses recently that I just haven't been able to because the founders don't know enough about the numbers. They can't give me straight answers. I go into Xero, and it's nonsense. So, I can't trust it. And if I can't trust it, I can't buy it. So, I think you need someone who's good with the finances there.

When we bought Elite, the seller didn't even have a lawyer. We built up such good credibility that he didn't bother involving a lawyer. We can just do it between ourselves. So, it's essentially done on a handshake. Now, we had a lawyer to paper everything. But I think that if you can find a seller that makes sense and you have a good relationship, you need to involve fewer and fewer people. The more people you have involved, the more everyone feels like they need to justify their fee. And they do that by adding barriers and extending the process. So, I think what I would say as a buyer is, don't feel you need to find a really expensive finance person, a really expensive lawyer, a really expensive commercial person, and a really expensive broker.

Actually, that doesn't have to be the case at all. All of those people will try to justify their existence by just adding work for the other side. And it may be the other side just gets fed up and walks off and goes to find another deal.

The other really annoying thing is that when the business owner has gone to the accountant to get a valuation, the accountant has absolutely no idea about valuations. So they've just made up some bullshit number which ends up being five times some ridiculously non-adjusted EBITDA and now the seller has the expectation, 'I'm going to get £10 million pounds for my business that's not doing anything like £2 million in profit'. It's particularly relevant because the profit drops even lower when you adjust for the cost of replacing the founder on all the jobs that they are doing. But because they've got that expectation in their heads, any reasonable offer from a legit buyer is going to fall on stony ground. So you've just got to be so careful. You've got to make yourself easy to buy, not difficult to buy.

*Ali: When should an owner not be thinking about selling?*

*Tim:* I remember once when I was in a really dark place with Exposure Ninja and I went to someone and said, 'I'm done,' and he gave me some really honest advice and said, 'Dude, don't sell now. Don't sell at the bottom. You're an idiot if you do it now'. And I'm so glad I took that advice.

Sometimes you feel like all you want to do is just get this thing off your plate, and if someone came along and offered you £100k for it, you'd just bite their hand off because you want to be free of it. And that's the worst time to sell. It really is. You've got to hold your nerve and sell when you least want to sell. Sell when it's healthy. Sell when it's looking great. It's really difficult to time the top, but when you're really excited about the future, when everything's going great, you've signed all these big clients and profits are amazing. Really, that's the time to sell. Don't wait until you're desperate.

* * *

## The Future

*Ali: What do you think the future of agencies looks like with AI?*

*Tim:* Absolutely no idea, and we've had this conversation at Exposure Ninja a lot. I actually don't think anybody knows. Even the people who are building these AI tools don't really know what they're capable of or what they're going to be capable of in the future. And anyone who tells you they know what's going to happen to the world of work, honestly doesn't. Nobody has any idea. We've never seen anything like this. So, I think all you can do is to be a few months ahead at any point.

*Ali: What does the future look like for you?*

*Tim:* I'm really enjoying building the renewables group; it's incredibly engaging. So, I want to do more of that. It's all driven by marketing and the agency, of course. The agency's growth is the thread that's going to run through whatever business we buy - using inbound leads. I'm really enjoying working at Elite. I'll hand that off to someone to run soon and then on to the next one, and the next one, and the next one.

No idea what the next five years is going to look like, but I've got no idea what the next six months is going to look like either, to be honest, but that's what I enjoy.

## Finding Tim Cameron-Kitchen

You can find Tim shinobicapital.co and by email at tim@shinobicapita l.co

* * *

> **Want to see how exit-ready your agency is?**
> *Take the 3-minute test:* ***agencyexits.co.uk/book***
>
> **Not selling yet?**
> *Now is a great time to build for the future.*
> *Book a call and I'll show you how to scale profitably, reduce founder dependency, and build a high-value agency on your*

> *terms.*
> ***agencyexits.co.uk/contact***

* * *

## Exit Story Takeaways

### 1. Complete before you exit

Tim didn't sell. He stepped back. Installing a CEO and full leadership team turned Exposure Ninja into a self-sufficient machine. You can't sell if you can't step back, so completion is the milestone every founder needs to reach first. Then you have the option of staying in the business, exploring new ideas or selling.

### 2. Sales dependency kills value

If the business lives and dies on your input, buyers won't touch it. Build a sales and marketing engine that works without you. Otherwise, you're just selling yourself. *(Ali: I can help you with this! agencyexits.com/call)*

### 3. A proper organisation chart beats a 'number two'

Delegating everything you don't want to do just shifts dependency. Rather than relying on an ops-critical lieutenant, Tim layered the management structure and built from the bottom up: department heads, a general manager, then a CEO. That's what makes a business scalable, sellable, and low-risk for buyers.

### 4. Sell when you don't feel like it

Tim was once advised not to sell when things felt darkest, and he's glad he listened. Selling at the bottom of a dip means pennies on the pound. The right time to sell is when you least want to, which is usually when things are healthy, profitable, and exciting.

### 5. Make yourself easy to buy

Messy numbers; overcomplicated brokerage; blind loyalty to inflated valuations. They'll all leave you watching as buyers walk away. Tim's deals move fast because they're simple, cash-generating, and founder-independent. That's what acquirers pay for.

# 6

# The Agency & The Work First

*"People knew the names who were a part of Frank,*
*but it was always agency and the work first."*
*— Andrew Bloch*

**Entrepreneur:** Andrew Bloch
**Exit Types & Timeline:**
Initial Sale & Uncapped Earn-out (2007)
End of Earn-out & Partial Return of Shareholding (2012)
Full Management Buy-back (2021)
Employee Ownership Trust (2024)
**Exited Agency:** Frank PR
**Exit Value:** Reported as Estimated Minimum of £17 million (PR Week, 2007)
Estimated Final Exit Value £25 million (Industry Insiders, 2011)
**Purchaser**: Photon Group (Later Renamed to Enero)

Andrew Bloch doesn't really do 'steady.' When he co-founded *Frank*

*PR*, his mission was simple (or, at least, it sounds simple): create a brand that people can't ignore. For Andrew, that was about more than winning flashy headlines (though *Frank* did become famous for doing exactly that). Really, it meant treating his own agency as a brand in its own right – loud, memorable, and impossible for the industry to overlook.

I first got to know Andrew at *Exposure Ninja* board meetings. From time to time, he'd pitch an idea that left me thinking: *damn, that's bold.* One of his ideas involved creating services that were fun first, profitable second. The logic? Inspire, excite, and engage potential clients right from the get-go. Then, support them with higher-value services a little way down the road.

The idea stayed with me. I came to think of it like a shop-window stunt: fun, exciting, designed to get attention. Not necessarily built to sell, but definitely built to *spark*. And once potential clients stepped inside the shop – *that's* when *Frank* could offer them the stuff they really needed.

While we were talking, what struck me was how different the approach was from other founders in this book. Where Mark and Luke crafted every brick with stonemason-like precision, and Dom blazed a trail into uncharted frontiers, Andrew's edge was pure brand theatre. He saw that a carefully designed name, a thoughtfully curated reputation, and a world-beater of a story would do the heavy lifting – bringing in clients, acquirers, and press, without Andrew (or anyone from *Frank*, for that matter) needing to spend a single moment on lead-gen.

His eventual buyout was the result of years spent turning *Frank* into a brand that people wanted to be associated with. If there's one thing I learned from Andrew *(Ali: there is more than one thing I learned from Andrew)*, it's this: you don't need a perfect plan, or to feel completely ready. If your brand's shop window is a thing of real beauty, opportunities will come knocking.

Here's the case in point.

* * *

## The Entrepreneur

### Origins

*Ali: To get us started, tell us how your career began and where you are now.*

*Andrew:* I started my career at an agency called Lynne Franks PR, which was one of the hottest agencies in the '90s. It was the inspiration for the TV show *Absolutely Fabulous.* It was a crazy place, and probably the best place I could have worked. I started there on a three-week work placement and got offered a job at the end.

That's where I met Graham Goodkind, who became my partner later down the line at Frank. About three years into my journey at Lynne Franks, the company got acquired by Ketchum, which was an Omnicom agency, and Graham was opposed to that acquisition. He felt the agency would lose its energy, what made it special, and get swallowed up by corporate culture. So he left and went off to start an internet company, which was the fashionable thing to do then, and I stayed. I felt that being part of Ketchum would give me experience of a big global agency, and I became head of sport and entertainment. I looked after these incredible accounts and had a brilliant experience. I loved every second of it.

One day, Graham knocked on my door and said, 'Fancy setting up an agency?'. He missed agency life, and it was 2000; the dotcom bubble had burst.

I said to him, 'Look, I don't feel ready.' He said, 'You'll never feel ready'. Which is advice that has stuck with me for many years, and advice I've given to hundreds of other people. There's never a good time to do these things. But also Graham didn't want to be the executive of the company. He was still involved in the internet company and wasn't planning to be particularly hands-on. He was MD when I was going through the ranks. So, he was more senior than me. So I told him I was up for it but that I'd like to do it with someone else involved. To cut a long story short, I found someone else. We had some backing from a marketing agency called Branded. We got off to a flying start. It was an accelerated startup. The first couple of clients were friends and family; then, our third client was Amstrad, which is owned by Lord Alan Sugar. Lord Sugar is still a client of mine 25 years later.

The marketing agency that backed us was about to be acquired themselves, and we became an inconvenience to them. So we managed to buy ourselves out from them. The big learning for me was that we didn't really need that investment, and certainly didn't need as much as we took. We had given up quite a lot of equity to get that money, but we were fortunate because we had become inconvenient to them, we could buy ourselves out.

Unfortunately, their deal fell through, but our deal was already done so we parted ways even though they never sold in the end.

After two or three years, we started to get offers for our company. We understood our value, but we weren't ready yet. It wasn't until year seven that we sold to an Australian PLC called Photon (later renamed to Enero). A few years into the earn-out, we ended up owning a portion of Frank again alongside them. Fast forward twenty years, and Enero still held the majority stake, with the management team retaining the balance. By then we were doing extremely well with offices all around the world, but I felt I had an entrepreneurial itch to scratch. So I moved into a non-exec role. It was a tough decision, and it took me a couple of years to make it.

Unlike some founders, I had made my money. I'm not saying that I didn't need to work again, and I definitely *wanted* to work again, but I wasn't living hand-to-mouth, which helped with my decision because I could do whatever I wanted and take my time about it. But the main thing was to figure out what I do and don't like, what I am good at, and what I am not good at. I've got an encyclopaedic knowledge of my industry; I don't enjoy writing; I don't like deep strategy and chin-scratching; and I don't enjoy employing people and having to deal with that. I'm a good communicator, and I'm creative and understand what makes a good story.

So then I put an announcement on LinkedIn to say what I was doing, and the phone started ringing immediately, and it was amazing really. Three weeks after my decision, COVID happened, which was obviously an unprecedented time. I was thinking, fuck, I've had 20 years to choose my timing, and this is the moment I've chosen. But I don't believe there's ever a good or a bad time to do anything. And change is good because people need advice and consultancy then.

These days my career falls into five buckets, all of which complement each other. The first is M&A. I head up the marketing services division at PCB Partners, working buy-side and sell-side. The second is in consultancy with brands. At AAR, I advise major brands on their agency ecosystems and run high-profile pitch processes for companies like Starbucks, Goldman Sachs and Greggs. The third is I am a NED and advisor to several marketing agencies. I have also invested in several businesses, like Stakked and I'm the co-founder of Big Dog Talent, which is a platform for booking celebrities, creators and influencers. The fourth is that I still work in PR and crisis communications. I've kept Lord Sugar as a PR client, managing his media profile and supporting every Apprentice winner since 2005. Lastly, I dedicate around 20% of my time to mentoring, education and charities, including The Kings

Trust, the School of Communication Arts, Grief Encounter, and Variety. So that's my portfolio career, really. I don't have any staff; I do all of it myself working along side best in class partners. It's me and the contacts in my little black book.

*Ali: Which of the five is your favourite?*

*Andrew:* It's such a good question. The bit that gives me pleasure is the diversity, which is a bit of a cop-out, but it's the same as when I was running an agency. I love that one day you're focused on hamburgers, the next it's cars, and the next it's the NHS. That's how my brain works. I get bored quickly, and I like to move from one thing to the next. I adore the M&A side because you're changing people's lives - without being too dramatic about it. That's unbelievable. But it takes a long time. Sometimes it feels a bit like you're an estate agent that's on a basic wage, and you're waiting to sell that house so that you can have a holiday.

I love working on the talent stuff. Yesterday I was speaking to a bank in the Middle East about an ad campaign they want to do. I reckon by the weekend, we'll have done a deal, and there's significant money involved, but it's a quick in and out type of project.

So it's a real mixture. What I learnt early on was to keep everything related so that it can feed into each other. I made a couple of mistakes along the way. I invested in a drinks company and a restaurant basically because I liked the branding and I like fried chicken. Those are not good reasons for investing in stuff. Stick to what you know.

Since then, I've honed my portfolio and been quite good at saying no. I wasn't particularly good at that in the past. Your most valuable commodity is your time. So, you've got to protect it at all costs. And trying to do things that all merge into one another really helps.

## Skills

*Ali: What are the skills that made you good at running an agency, and being able to deal with the chaos that comes with that?*

*Andrew:* Time management, the ability to differentiate between what's urgent and what's important, resilience and staying sane, are the biggest skill sets you can have. In PR, you've got to know the basics – writing, speaking, and tech. After that, it's your resilience, client skills, and creativity that really matter. It's about understanding the media, the landscape, and how it works. It's not a 9-5 job. So if you're looking for an easy life, it's probably not the career for you.

So for me, I think it's resilience, creativity, and determination. I don't think there's a single founder in this world who isn't determined, who hasn't put in the weekend shifts, who hasn't dealt with issues. And I think running an agency is like spinning plates. And they're always spinning and they're always wobbling. You've just got to make sure that a plate doesn't fall off and smash and hit the floor. And if it does, you have to figure out how you can pick it up and start spinning it again. When you look at the agency world, you're looking at people's show reels, and it all looks fantastic, all glossy, all brilliant work, and happy people. When you're advising an agency or you're running an agency, you're dealing with the behind-the-scenes video, and it's the tears, the tantrums, the lost clients, the director who's just walked out, and the person who's just gone on maternity leave unexpectedly and left a huge gap. That is running an agency.

They call it the souffle effect. Agencies sort of puff up, get to a certain size, and then they deflate a bit and then they puff up again. You just have to accept that it's not a smooth ride.

When I was running my agency, I don't know whether it was unusual, but we had more or less nine to ten years of consistent growth. And then, for various reasons, we hit a wall. We didn't crash down to earth, but suddenly things stabilised and went flat, and in certain areas they declined, and that was my true test. It's lovely and very easy when everything's going right and you're going in the right direction. The test of strength is when it's not. So, and that served me well now advising other agencies because I think if you've never dealt with adversity, you can't help other people deal with it.

* * *

## Building The Agency

### Development

*Ali: Tell me a bit about Frank PR and how it was different when it started to what it became.*

*Andrew:* The world is not waiting for another PR agency, and so you need a point of differentiation and to stand for something. When I look back at Frank, and everything it's achieved to date, I think its point of differentiation and strength as a brand was probably one of its greatest successes. If you've got a powerful brand and a strong culture, you attract the right clients; you do the right work; you get the best people, and it's a sort of virtuous circle.

The name Frank was my name, and we landed on it after lots and lots of debate. It came from being open, honest, and no bullshit, which reflected the characters of the three of us that founded it. It was also a play on Lynne Franks and mine and Graham's heritage. And Lynne Franks was one of the greatest creative agencies of its era, completely defining in terms of what it achieved. We wanted to keep the best bits of that alive. But PR often has a bad reputation for being fluffy and not strategic. My experience at a big agency was super positive, but I felt it was a bit corporate, and wasn't direct enough in that there weren't enough senior people doing the work. I wanted to get rid of all of that when we started Frank.

We also had this principle of 'talkability'. So it was never about doing work for the sake of it; it was about creating a reaction to get people talking. When we started Frank it was in the early days of the internet, so talkability to us meant around the water cooler or the black cab driver test. It was work that would get people noticed, and get people talking about you to effectively do your best marketing for you. So talkability was a big part of the ethos of Frank. We trademarked the word and created a proprietary methodology around it. It was our guiding light and still is to this day.

## Growth

*Ali: An agency with a few people is very different to manage than a big one, because the ideas can get more diffuse and the team feel less connected to each other. How did you maintain the culture as the agency grew?*

*Andrew:* Yeah, exactly. I think one of the biggest skills of running an agency is becoming a big agency without losing what made you special in the first place. I think it's partly a mindset piece because when you have a lot of people; you think you've got to put in processes and systems, and that can destroy a culture. Obviously, you have to put some processes and systems in place because suddenly it's a bigger entity, which is harder to manage, but you don't have to lose what made you special in the first place. Like a lot of agencies, we grew up and got to a certain size and then thought, 'Oh, we're boring now. We've grown up too much,' and then we stripped it away.

One of our early clients was a recruitment business, and the CEO was a guy called Lawrence Rosen, who used to talk about pillows, and he said, 'You never want too many pillows in an organisation'. At first, I didn't understand what he meant by it. But what he meant was, don't put in too many soft things that don't make a difference and are just an expense. Keep it lean; don't put in meetings for the sake of meetings; don't introduce hierarchies you don't need; keep the fundamental decision-making with the people that made the agency what it was in the first place. So, I think Frank, like a lot of successful agencies, has kept that culture and that fun. Even when we were owned by someone else, it felt like our agency. And if you'd have asked people who worked there, often they wouldn't have even known that the agency had been sold. So it was that was keeping that culture alive.

*Ali: What did new business look like?*

*Andrew:* I was a great believer that it was all about the work. If you're doing great work consistently, you will always attract the right clients and the right people. We pushed ourselves so hard for best-in-class creativity that we'd often rule out things that would have probably won Cannes Lions. We were so tough on ourselves, but it was the right thing to do.

One of my roles in the agency until the very last day that I was there was to promote the agency and to keep the buzz alive. I was a great believer in doing your own PR because that's the visibility. Some of that came from a fear of doing new business. I did not want to be on the phone having to beg for clients. I wanted clients to come to us.

I didn't want to build a new business department or do it myself. And I believed we should attract like-minded clients. So by doing great work, pushing it out, the type of clients that wanted that work would naturally come to us. So that was a real driving motivator. Lots of people tried to copy our style of marketing, and that was flattering. It's now quite a big part of most agencies, but we were always one step ahead in how we were doing it. I've seen, admired, and worked with great entrepreneurs like Steven Bartlett who have built their agencies more on themselves and their personal brand, which was not something Frank did. People knew the names who were a part of Frank, but it was always agency and the work first.

* * *

# The Exit

## Preparation

*Ali: Did you always think you would exit one day?*

*Andrew:* Yes and no. When we started, I came from a position of failure as an entrepreneur, as I'm quite risk-averse. So, for me, I needed to go through the process of thinking about what's the worst that can happen? If we don't get the clients, I'll go back to my old job with my cap in hand, or I'll find something else. So it's not the end of the world. That was it, really. I just wanted us to survive and to get through the first year. Which we did, we were doing PR for a business called Startle, which was a spin-off of Telstar. We were working from a swanky office in Chelsea, which was not very us, but it was free in exchange for PR, and it was great. And then suddenly the office owners had gone into liquidation, so we went in one day and there were removers taking the computers off our desks and we were like, 'Shit!'. So we found a place in Chalk Farm, which was a lot more 'us'. At that stage though, you never think one day we're going to be worth tens of millions of pounds.

But we were always very disciplined about how we did our accounts, how we planned, held ourselves accountable and gave our teams KPIs. So it was always there in our minds. The first people started coming to us with offers about 3 years in. It was at that point we started to understand how they were working out our value. We started thinking about it as, 'Okay, for every pound we make, they will give us five or six pounds; therefore we're worth this much money'. Suddenly, you've got something tangible, and you work out what the number is that you want, and you push for it. Then, you start to see if you can increase the multiplier because that increases the number too. So as soon as we understood the valuation metrics, we had a figure in our mind and felt that when we hit that number it would be the right time to sell.

*Ali: Were you then prospecting for buyers or did they come to you?*

*Andrew:* This is where luck comes into things, in that we didn't particularly want to go to market, but we knew we had to get our books perfect so that we would be ready for a sale. So we went to see several firms. We liked one. We came back from that meeting and, no word of a lie, that afternoon he phoned my partner and said, 'Look, this is a bit weird, but we've got this client in Australia who's over in London. They're looking at agencies. They might like you. Do you want to go and meet them?'. And my partner agreed. He met them, and it was like one of those scenes in a movie where they write a figure on a napkin and shove it across a table in a hotel. My partner came back from that meeting and we thought, 'Fuck, big number'. It was more than we'd thought - and that was their starting offer.

## Negotiation

*Ali: What can you tell us about the deal?*

*Andrew:* Through that hotel meeting, we'd found our perfect acquirer. They were then called Photon and are now called Enero. We believe it was probably the greatest PR exit that has ever been achieved in our working era.

It was a phenomenal deal. We liked them. They were great people. But one of the most important things with any deal, which I think a lot of founders don't understand, is that timing is everything. You don't want to sell when you're at your peak. You don't want to sell when you're flat because you're not attractive. You certainly don't want to sell when you're declining because you will not get your value.

We structured a deal that was an uncapped earn-out based on growth from our starting base. And in the four years that came after the initial consideration, we flew. It was a super motivating time because every pound you're making is worth X and there's someone that's written a guarantee that they're going to pay that. So, we worked our ass off, and that was the golden era of the agency. I'd never worked so hard. The people had never worked so hard, and we got a payment after two years. After four years, they had done a load of deals like this. I think there were 35 deals in the space. I think they'd bought some stuff that didn't do well, and they lost money, did some deals that were doing okay, and that they bought a few like Frank that were flying. So suddenly I think they were in a position where they had to pay out more than they had expected, and they couldn't afford it.

My impression was that it got to a stage where they were almost going to go under if we didn't accept an offer from them. We'd already had our first and second payments, but I think they couldn't afford to pay what they owed us on our last instalment. Now, for us, it was always the cherry on the icing on the cake. We were never expecting it, but even so, once you know you're owed it, you want it. But we ended up doing a deal where we got a third of the last portion in cash, a third of it in shares in Enero, and then they gave a third of the value back to us as equity in Frank. So that's how we came to own back a portion of the company.

*(Ali: A note to help with the timelines here: Frank PR was originally sold to Photon (now Enero) in 2007. In 2012, Andrew and the management team were given back part of the agency as a means of ending the earn-out. Then, in 2021, a full management buyout returned Frank to complete independence. Finally, in 2024, the shareholders sold the business to its employees as an Employee Ownership Trust (EOT).)*

There was nothing we could do about it; we couldn't do a lot else. It was a case of take what you can get or you're going to get nothing, and they weren't calling our bluff. It was a horrible time, and it was genuine. But when I look back at it, I sold my shares in Enero when they were at a decent level, and I got what I would have got in cash, anyway. I think it was slightly under, but not dramatically.

I have equity in Frank off the back of that deal. I would never have had those otherwise, and they have gone on to realise a lot of value. I think things would have looked very different had that not have happened because, as in most deals, we were just hoping for the best with an earn-out. You hope to achieve what you think you can, but then you get to the end of that period (*if* you get to the end of that period) and see what's there. A lot of founders do the first part of the deal, and then they can see that they will not hit the earn-out targets. So, what's the point of sticking around for another couple of years?

If you're an acquirer, and it's a trade deal, you want to tie in the senior people for a time because that's the thing with agencies, it's all reliant on the people. Frank didn't do it deliberately, but there were and still are two or three people at the top who are critical to its success. So if you take that away, then it's a significant part of the value of the agency. An acquirer wants to tie those people in, but also to make sure there's a next tier of management that are just as good, if not better, and younger, and hungrier. They want them tied in with equity, and motivated so they can go through the same process themselves. And that's where a lot of deals go wrong for both the acquirer and the seller.

We were very lucky. You could say you make your own luck. I'm not being super self-deprecating and humble, but we got lucky. A lot of events happened along the way that just made it a phenomenal deal. Like I said, I genuinely believe it was the best deal ever done in the PR industry. So, something to be proud of, I guess. Maybe more luck than judgment, but that's what we achieved.

*Ali: There's always a bit of both luck and judgement though, isn't there? So, on the note of creating your own luck, what are the things that you're really glad you had put in place?*

*Andrew:* When you're selling or buying, it's a risk-reward equation that you're trying to figure out. So, people are important; culture is important. We knew who we wanted to sell to and who we didn't. And that was more to do with the way we would be managed rather than about any specific organisation. But entrepreneurs don't want to be micromanaged. They've built a company and a culture. They don't want to be part of a big organisation. Some do, but most don't. You have to know what you want. For us, Enero is based on the other side of the world, and they're a PLC. The board at the time also weren't marketing experts. So, for us, that was a real bonus. It was the right type of culture, and just the time difference on its own meant, how hands-on could they be? They were as far away as they could be. That was a big incentive for us.

They bought into the senior people in the agency, but they didn't really ask us about our next-tier management or our succession planning. I mean, we didn't have any succession planning. I guess the fact that my partner is still there today shows that we loved it. We weren't looking to sit on a desert island with our slippers on, smoking a pipe, waiting to die. That wasn't the dream.

We had sensible things prepared. Our numbers were impeccable, and we'd run the company responsibly. We didn't run it like a lifestyle business. If you do, it doesn't mean you can't sell it, but it's that bit more complicated when you have to go through due diligence. We paid our taxes, took normal salaries, and we weren't putting loads of personal expenses through the company that weren't really business expenses. So that helped. The intangible factor is that we had an amazing brand. We were super hot and a defining agency of our era. So, that made a big difference to the company that was buying us. Having that magic fairy dust can make a massive difference to the valuation of the deal.

We weren't obsessed with selling the business. We were obsessed with running a brilliant business. That was important when we got into the deal. It's distracting, and it's hard work, especially when the buyer is on the other side of the world and you've got a horrible time difference. My partner's wife worked in the city, and she was our finance director for the period of the deal. She's a genius and consequently was massively overqualified. We couldn't have done the deal without her because it allowed us to get on with running the business. She did the horrible bit in terms of the legals and numbers; the things I'd never been good at and have certainly never enjoyed.

I remember going into the lawyer's office, and the paperwork was the length of a football pitch. We signed it all, and the lawyer got out the champagne and handed it around, saying, 'Come on, let's go on a night out and celebrate'. And we said, 'Sorry, we've got a pitch tomorrow'.

So, me and Graham went back to the office and worked on the pitch. I can't even remember if we won it. But that was our mentality. Business as usual, and we never really stopped and reflected that much. The first time I really reflected was when I was stepping down.

*Ali: It's really interesting. I spoke to an agency just the other day that came to me because they want to exit. Everything about them sounded brilliant, but they were almost putting it off. They wanted to get moving, but also were concerned about things that were 98% ready, but not 100%. The trouble is, it's never going to be 100% ready, and in the meantime you need to start building your network and figuring out who might buy this thing.*

*It sounds as though you almost had the same thing with the succession planning where you could have said that you needed to wait for that. But instead, you went for it.*

*Andrew:* I think so many agencies wait too long, and what an acquirer wants is growth. If you plateau, you might think that it's great that you've got a stable company that does a million pounds every year, but to succeed they need you to be making £1 million, then £1.1 million, then £1.2 million. So if you wait too long, you might go stagnant, or worse, decline.

In our case, someone came to us. We could have been greedy and thought, 'We're doing really well. We'll wait another year'. But if we had waited a year, who knows what would have happened? We sold our business in September 2007. The financial crash came very, very shortly after. And had that have happened to us, I'm sure we would have sold at some point, but it would have probably delayed the deal by a few years. So sometimes you have just got to take the bird in the hand. Hindsight's wonderful, and it was definitely the right thing for us. I can't tell you we knew it at the time, but our instinct was that we would never get a better deal and so we should grab it with both hands.

*Ali: A lot of founders* wait *until they're almost burnt out and they feel like they can't do it anymore. You weren't at that point. You were very much still in the, 'I love my business,' phase.*

*Andrew:* That's so true. No one wants to buy a burnt-out founder. No one wants to buy someone who's about to retire unless there's a great team underneath them. We were full of energy. I'm never going to be ready to retire. I think I'll be wheeled into a coffin from my office desk. But when we were selling, I was in my 30s, and I don't want to be too crass about it, but I'd paid off every debt I'd had, bought a beautiful house, got a flash car, and put my kids through private school. But that was never my motivation. I was young, hungry, motivated, and even now I'm supposed to be taking it easy, but I'm not. I'm working with exactly the same energy, if not more than I had 5 years ago, because I love it. And that's what someone's looking to buy.

They don't want the stressed founder. You don't want to have a distressed sale. I deal with a lot of distressed sales, and there's still a satisfaction in receiving a value for them because the founder has almost given up - so they see getting anything as an excellent result. But I always say, 'Dig deep'. It's better to wait a year and not be desperate because it would make a big difference. Sometimes people take that advice, and sometimes they don't. It's not necessarily that my advice is right or wrong; if someone just wants out, then you try to do the best deal you can, but I'd rather sell a business that's flying.

*Ali: What's really interesting to me is that a lot of exited founders I speak to have a sense of grief after the sale because their phone has suddenly stopped ringing, they've stopped getting emails and no one needs them. Your story sounds quite different in that you reached a point where you were moving towards doing something and were excited about being more entrepreneurial. Why do you think it was different for you?*

*Andrew:* I never lost the entrepreneurial feeling or the emotional connection to my firm. That was because the acquirer didn't want us to lose the emotional connection. They wanted us to walk in everyday feeling like it was still our agency. You could call us naïve, but we bounced into work still feeling like it was ours because they gave us autonomy. They checked in, and if we weren't hitting numbers, trust me, they were on it. But as long as things were going in the right direction, they enjoyed seeing the work, but they didn't really care.

So I never felt any grief because I was still busy. I think you need to have a sense of purpose in your career, and I've still got that.

*Ali: It's interesting to look at it from a buyer's perspective too. When you're working with buy-side clients, what are they looking for?*

*Andrew:* A lot of our buy-side clients have very specific acquisition needs, which might be by skill set, it might be by geography, or it could be bulking up an existing skill set. So certain areas are in high demand, and so it's harder to find the best companies. So, data is a popular area; influencer marketing; digital marketing; healthcare PR; and consumer PR is booming at the moment. The buyer doesn't want any old dross that's on the market. They don't want to be involved in an auction process where they're bidding against their competitors.

If they're looking to bulk up their skill sets, then they are looking for companies that are very, very similar in terms of size, culture, and the type of work they do, so they can bulk up for a private equity sale or to a trade organisation that needs to increase their share value.

* * *

## The Future

*Ali: What's next for you?*

*Andrew:* I don't really have a five-year plan. It's more of the same. My metric for life is now whether I wake up and get out of bed with a smile on my face, and as long as I'm happy and enjoying it - I don't question it too much. It makes me sound like I'm the village idiot. And of course we all have good days, and bad days. But genuinely, if I'm mentally stimulated and I'm really enjoying it, then that's enough for me. I love buying and selling agencies, and being in a position where I can change people's lives is a privilege and one I don't take for granted. I'm very lucky.

### Finding Andrew Bloch

You can find Andrew at andrewbloch.co.uk

* * *

> ***agencyexits.co.uk/contact***

* * *

## Exit Story Takeaways

**1. Timing is everything**

Andrew sold just before the financial crash. A year later, valuations tanked. You can't predict the future, but you can keep an ear to the ground. When momentum, market interest, and agency energy align, that's your green light. Make your move then.

**2. Hot agencies get hot valuations**

Frank wasn't just a profit machine. It was 'the agency of its era'. We see it time and time again: buyers pay a premium for buzz. Keep your brand razor-sharp and make sure it's being talked about – it adds serious money to your multiple.

**3. Get your house in order**

Clean numbers, proper salaries, and no lazy 'lifestyle' expenses. Andrew stresses that due diligence is brutal and any shortcuts you take will cost you later. Build it as if you'll be audited tomorrow, and you're likely to be more profitable whether you choose to sell or stay.

**4. Don't wait until you're burnt out**

Andrew sold at a point of strength. He was energised, engaged, and still in love with the business. Buyers don't want a founder who's checked out. The best deal happens when you could stay, but choose to go.

**5. Fortune favours the... prepared**

The 'napkin deal' with an Australian buyer looks like luck, but it landed because Frank was sale-ready, scalable, and attractive. Stack the odds by building an agency with real curb appeal – the type of agency buyers have to have, with a clear proposition and a strong brand reputation. Being prepared is how you make your own luck.

# III

# Frontier Thinking

# 7

# Gold Rush

We've seen the beauty of structure, sales, leads and planning. Not everything can be meticulously planned when the world is in a state of flux. With the AI evolution moving at a faster rate than anything we have ever seen, I believe we are in one such state of flux. These times need planning and flexibility in equal measure. The area you thought would be big might be gone tomorrow. The bet your competitor took just might pay off.

Despite AI being a new and daunting challenge for agencies to adapt to, we can still learn lessons from the past. In the next chapter, we will hear from Dominic McGregor, co-founder of Social Chain, which is most commonly known as Steven Bartlett's agency and debut into the business world. Dominic was right there alongside him from day one, and together they filled different roles within the company.

You'll hear Dom talk about how they were in the right place at the right time and read the tea leaves with precision at the dawn of social media. They developed quickly by constantly evaluating which platform they needed to dominate next - and where they needed to stop spending their time and energy. It meant that while process and structure were needed, they could not allow them to be shackles that prevented movement and adaptation.

As we try to capitalise on the next frontier, the one that some like to call agencies' last, we can learn from Dom how to seize our moment and build something that is designed for exit - even when the world is in a state of flux.

# 8

# Diamonds & Social Chain

*"How do you see the relationship between pressure and achievement?"*
*"That's how diamonds are formed."*
*– Dominic McGregor.*

**Entrepreneur:** Dominic McGregor
**Exit Type:** IPO (via reverse merger / public listing)
**Exited Agency:** Social Chain (The Social Chain AG)
**Time to Exit:** 5 years to IPO | 6 years from founding
**Exit Value:** Public listing no single sale price disclosed. The company later upgraded to Frankfurt's Prime Standard (2021); reporting referenced an approximate US$600m valuation at that stage.
**Employees at Exit:** 750

Every gold rush has its heroes. In the last big frontier moment – the dawn of social media – Steven Bartlett (you may have heard of him) played the role of public figurehead, while his co-founder Dominic McGregor was in the engine room, quietly keeping the rocket ship from blowing apart on the launchpad.

And it really was a rocket ship. Together, they took Social Chain from a student side-hustle to a $300m turnover global agency, IPO and all, working with brands like Apple and Amazon before most agencies had ever even gained a blue tick or sent their first retweet.

More than good old-fashioned hustle and hype, Dom's story shows what happens when youth, timing and conviction collide – and the equally important moment you realise you need to bring in a senior team to stop the whole thing from capsizing at scale. He loved his subject, interpreted the tea leaves of the social frontier better than most, and never stopped adapting. That's the fuel that allowed Social Chain to hit escape velocity.

Why does this matter now? Because we're staring down the barrel of a new *(Ali: final?)* frontier that's just as wild and unpredictable: the age of AI.

Agency owners who treat AI the way Social Chain treated early social – as a moving target to chase, not a force of nature to react to – will strike gold. Meanwhile, those that cling to the old ways will be fossilised before they can say: *does that look like a meteor to you?*

Dom's journey is an exhibition in capitalising on frontier moments and building towards your own exit story.

* * *

## The Entrepreneur

## Origins

*Ali: To get us started, tell us how your career began.*

*Dom:* I guess let's go back to what my hopes and dreams were because I started so early; I didn't yet have a career to talk about. I wanted to go into sports science. So I studied it at university, and my dream was to be in football. I love football. I love sport. So that was my priority. That was also the time when Facebook had just become very popular, so when you went to university all of your friends from home were on Facebook with you and then you'd make new friends. There was also the emergence of platforms like Instagram and Twitter. So I spent a lot of time on social media just connecting and talking to friends from back home, and while I was at university, I probably spent too much time on social media. I also did a couple of jobs around them. I worked at Vodka Revolutions and at AMT Coffee Bar, but I never really had any intentions of going into business, or any plans other that to go to university to play football and try to get into sports. That's what I had been wanting to do since I was about five, so that was my career before it all started.

*Ali: So how did you and Steven Bartlett end up starting Social Chain? I've read that it was a bit of an accident.*

*Dom:* I was running Twitter accounts, and the first one I started was called 'Student Problems', which was following my life at university. So I'd post about relatable student problems, for example, realising how expensive cheese is or posting memes. Twitter posts were limited to only 140 characters, or 140 characters and an image then. It could be I'm biased and I've post-rationalised it, because people always say they were straight on a new trend when it happened, but when Twitter introduced images, I was straight on there with funny pictures. I'd take pictures of friends, or post about my interests like Harry Potter, and I'd put funny captions on them – I didn't know that they would become called memes, I was just doing it because I thought they were funny.

I grew that student audience and then met Steve, who was running a business called Wallpark which was a student messaging board on a website. We tried to send traffic to the website from our student-focused social media pages, and that was the initial relationship. From there, we spoke to brands about advertising on the website and how we could send traffic to it from social media. We found brands were more interested in our social media presence than being on the website because our follower numbers were so high, and fewer people would click through onto the website than would see the post. That was an 'Aha!' moment for us. If we doubled down on social and got rid of the website, which was a blocker, then we could get more brands to work with us.

That was where the business was born. The logic behind the name Social Chain was that it was built on a chain of social media pages. We realised in hindsight that there were two routes we could have gone down. The first was the LADbible route which was editorial articles and AdSense, and ours was probably the more complicated route, which was trying to solve client problems by speaking to businesses and selling them concepts and creative campaigns to help them, rather than generating website traffic. We put less focus on the student forum website and focused entirely on social media. We started speaking to businesses that were trying to train students, and that was the start of our offering businesses our services to help them – which, if you break it down, is us starting an agency – although we didn't know that then.

*Ali: So you started off by having fun with memes on* Twitter, *and it turned into an agency!*

*Dominic:* Yeah, it was just a bit of fun. We were running social media accounts in bedrooms and starting worldwide trends. I remember starting a trend during the 2014 World Cup when Germany beat Brazil, and it got over two billion impressions on the trend that we just came up with in our bedrooms. So, the ability to influence people became our day-one product. All our pages would talk about something at once, and it would feel like it had come out of nowhere. That was our first service.

## Mindset

*Ali: You were both so young when you accidentally started an agency. I'm curious, how do you think you and Steven shaped each other's development?*

*Dom:* We had no previous experience in anything. Neither of us had ever worked in an office. So, when it came to things like building an office, we had no idea what it should look like. It meant that we built everything from our perspective as two young people. So, we put in a room that was literally just mats you could sleep on. We put in a bar and a jungle gym. We put in loads of stupid things that were intentionally there to keep people in the office. I think part of what made it so different was that we lived in the moment rather than based on any pre-conceptions of what an office should be. Neither of us had much business experience beyond watching *The Apprentice* on TV and seeing what Lord Alan Sugar was doing on there.

That was our starting point, and we had a blank canvas in front of us. That really changes your approach to problems because you have no prejudice based on what has been done before. So you ask, 'What should we do?' rather than saying, 'Oh, I've seen this before'. That was our entire approach to everything from our office to our own marketing and to how we approached client work. I remember learning about

Google Analytics for the first time. It was probably a year or so into working in a business that drives traffic to your website, yet I'd never heard of it. We were learning everything as we went, so there was a rawness and authenticity in our work when we started, which I think was the best advantage to us.

*Ali: It's interesting because you started by unknowingly solving a problem, rather than by figuring out what you could sell.*

*Dom:* We also just didn't know that we were different. We believed in what we did because we'd see it with our own eyes. We were disciples of it because we knew how quickly you could grow audiences and how young people were engaging with it. We hadn't been thinking about it in terms of the role of traditional marketing, because this is the route that we knew. We had hacked social media for so long that we knew it was a great decision and so we never got distracted by thinking, 'Oh you could buy clicks on Google, or use SEO,' because we knew this worked and how to do it.

*Ali: How do you see the relationship between pressure and achievement?*

*Dom:* That's how diamonds are formed.

***

## Building The Agency

## Development

*Ali: Who were your first clients?*

*Dom:* Some of our first clients were actually quite big names. Our first paying client was Pretty Little Thing, our second was a business selling university gift boxes called HelloU, and our third was Spotify. So we had two future unicorns, though they weren't unicorns at the time. Back then, they were mid-size businesses and focused on the student market. It made for a good story arc because we could then stand beside who we worked with very early. Having those names straight away meant we didn't have to focus on small regional businesses. I mean no disrespect to Tommy's Food Shack or whatever, but we were thinking straight away about national and global businesses rather than regionals. The interesting thing I see about a lot of agencies now is that when they're looking for work, they look for businesses around them. Having the big boys as clients from day one made us really confident. The thinking at 19 years old was that if we can get Spotify as our third paying client, then we can probably get any client.

*Ali: How much of that confidence came from not knowing any different? No one had ever told you that you couldn't or that it would be hard, and you were coming into it fresh.*

*Dom:* I think it's partly because we were disruptive, but also we had a product with assets, because we had audiences. Some great agencies are born without having a product and a service, but we were an agency with a product attached. So that made us appealing to everyone, and it was a significant reason to talk to us. If we had started by just selling social media services, we probably still would have got somewhere because of our timing, but we had an extra reason for people to talk to us.

*Ali: How much of your growth do you attribute to the brands you got at the start growing with you and you being able to mutually grow your businesses?*

*Dom:* Not as much as you might think because a lot of times we were focused on project work rather than campaigns. So, those early clients weren't really ones that we could land and then expand. From our perspective, that was fine in the beginning because when you go from earning nothing to people putting 20 to 30 grand in front of you for a campaign, you make hay while the sun shines! We also didn't have the resources then either. Because agencies are such people-based businesses, the in-and-out model suited us fine. It also worked well because social media was in its early days, and so the budgets businesses were using with us were experimental. There were no RFPs or budgets assigned at this point because social media agencies barely existed yet.

So our growth aligned with the growth of the sector, rather than with the growth of clients. So it was a case of a rising tide as much as anything.

*Ali: What do you think was your biggest blind spot as a founder when you were first developing the agency?*

*Dom:* That has a very easy answer. Our biggest blind spot was I thought we knew how to run a business because we were experts in our product. Most founders are product experts; they understand their space very well. What we didn't have expertise in was how to scale the company, and we thought we could do both. It felt very alien to think about getting someone into our social media business who had no experience in social media. It was only after tripping up a few times that we realised we needed to get someone in who knew how to scale and run a company.

From a founder perspective, what you need is to be free to focus on what's valuable. In our case, that was marketing, branding and the client work. So we needed to remove the problems that would take us away from that. So areas like finance, HR, recruitment and people problems were all much better being run by someone who has much more experience in those areas.

## Growth

*Ali: What was the catalyst for realising you needed help managing the business?*

*Dom:* To be honest, it was my drinking. At 23, I realised I was drinking too much. That in itself isn't unusual at a young age, but the issue is context. When alcohol interferes with your responsibilities, and when it holds back your career or your life, that's the moment you have to face it and do something about it.

For probably a year, Steve and I were sleepwalking into a few problems with the business. We were living together. He was on the second floor; and I was on the third. We didn't really talk about what was going on for either of us until it was too late. I kind of imploded, and that was in July 2016.

After that, we had a conversation; we needed to bring people in around us to help. The business was in a really healthy state, making good money, but we couldn't do it all alone. It was getting all-consuming. So we decided we needed proper expertise and people who had been there and done it to join the management team and support us. By November, we'd started making our first senior hires. Looking back, it says a lot about the state we were in that one founder could literally implode and the business would still be okay. It probably says quite a lot about the resilience of the model given that a business needs to be driven by the founders, but we were still in a good place.

I think it's because we had based the business on some good fundamentals. Our margins in the early days were great. Social media attracted young talent, so salaries were relatively low. A 'big' salary might have been £30k, but most of our team were on £21–22k, doing work they genuinely loved. They were being paid to do what they'd happily be doing for fun, and that translated into really healthy margins.

2016 was a real inflection point for us. Businesses started to increase their social media budgets significantly. That year we won a £250k campaign for Huawei, which delivered close to an 80% margin. It proved the model, gave us capital reserves, and showed we could really go after it. The challenge was cash flow. Clients like Amazon were on 90-day payment terms, so we'd sometimes be laying out £30k before seeing a penny back. The tension between margin and cash flow was constant.

Our work was also becoming more complex. The first campaign we did with Spotify had 100% margin – it was literally just us posting on our own social channels. But by 2016 we were integrating influencers, paid media, and even social retainers. The projects were bigger and more sophisticated, which meant lower margins and longer waits to get paid. The more we stacked bigger projects and bigger clients, the longer the payment terms became and the lower the margin because you can't get a 90% margin on a million-pound campaign because the project is more complex. So, that margin is obviously going to come down over time.

*Ali: How did you maintain the team culture as you scaled? A small team is pretty different to the hundreds of staff that you ended up with.*

*Dom:* Yeah, maintaining the culture was a priority for us, and we considered it completely non-negotiable. When you strip it back, our product was people. So we had to make sure we had the best people, and the happiest people. It was just the priority – no two ways about it.

Of course, this was back when everyone was in the same room every day, which made it easier to manage. You could see everyone, spot problems early, and keep a tight feedback loop. You could change things in the moment. If someone looked a bit down, you could do something that same day to lift them.

I think that was one of our strongest traits. We could hire great people, often pay them slightly less because of the culture and perks, attract them to the mission, and then their energy became infectious.

*Ali: What was the mission you attached people to in the early days?*

*Dom:* What made it easy for us was that we could create a rival. We were trying to prove that social media was the future, so we slandered TV, we slandered print, and all the old channels that felt 'against us'. Every good mission needs an enemy, and that was ours.

It resonated because the world was already shifting. Netflix was on the rise, and people were asking themselves, 'Do you even watch TV any more?'. Then we'd point out how much money was still going into TV versus social and how ridiculous that was. As a pitch, it was powerful. You create the enemy; and you have a product that people already believe in because they're living it every day, and that became the mission.

*Ali: The business had to evolve so much to get from start-up in a student house to Initial Public Offering. In that time, what was the most unpopular decision that you made that turned out to be the right one?*

*Dom:* Good question. There's one that stands out in hindsight. It never fully manifested, but it was something I had 100% conviction in and everyone else resisted. In some ways, it was the beginning of the end for me.

In 2019, we launched this little company from China in the UK called TikTok. We did their marketing strategy, got creators onboarded for them, and my message to the team off the back of that was: forget Facebook, forget everything else, and double down entirely on TikTok. I told them: you should literally down tools on the other platforms and focus your whole time on TikTok, because this is the future.

Obviously there was pushback, and that was from the audience perspective, from the social media management team, from strategy. I sent out the memo, but people didn't believe me. We were so slow in responding. By the time I was validated, I was already out of the business. And honestly, that was one reason I knew I wanted to leave. I couldn't get people to change direction, because the team had KPIs tied to growth on Facebook or YouTube or whatever, and pivoting to TikTok just wasn't in their psyche. That was the moment I realised the business had become structured and organised to the point the entrepreneurial spark and the 'just-get-it-done' mentality had gone.

We had an innovation team though, and they grew to a million followers on TikTok in three or four weeks because TikTok was boosting our posts. They were asking us which ones to promote. I remember thinking: we will never again have a situation where a platform works this closely with us. TikTok even paid us to create content. It was just a small £3k campaign for educational posts, but because it was small, the team said, 'No, we can't do it'. And I was saying: 'You don't understand, we've got a platform that's going to dominate, and they're giving us money and attention - we need to take it seriously'. But the computer kept saying no. I was forceful about it, but by then people just wanted more budget and more hires, whereas I wanted us to allocate time.

Eventually, I was proved right, but it felt like a slog. The opportunity was obvious, but I was fatigued.

I remember the first TikTok influencer campaign we sold. We used a girl called Lori L and she was a dancer on TikTok. We ran it for DreamWorks Studios. We probably charged DreamWorks around £70k, and our influencer costs were about £5k total. The reach of influencers on TikTok then was incredible, and the price was low because it was new and emerging. I kept saying, 'Let's build relationships with all this TikTok talent, and sell this product hard'. But everyone was still saying, 'No, let's stick with Instagram'. Meanwhile, Instagram prices were inflating, and margins were shrinking. I just wanted us to move on to the new thing and make it work.

*Ali: That must have felt so frustrating, and quite a departure from the original fluidity of Social Chain.*

*Dom*: Yes, my view is that if I were to make another service-based business straight after the Social Chain exit, it would have been a TikTok agency. I'd have gone straight on it because I knew it was the future.

The problem is we created a structure where people were focused on performance. They had stretch targets that were linked to the exit we were aiming for. People were getting share options tied to what they had to achieve, so it then didn't work to suddenly say, 'Forget that, focus on TikTok instead', because people just aren't wired that way.

We quickly realised that people need frameworks and guidance. I don't. I can just figure out what I want to do; I've always been like that. But most people want structure, progression, to know when they're doing a good job. I still don't know to this day if I'm doing a good job in anything I do; and I don't really care. You probably see that with all the stuff around people who have 'high agency'. You can self-refer, you can tell yourself you're doing well, you're maybe even a bit deluded sometimes, but you don't need someone else to validate what you're doing.

That's the hardest part for me. I started the company based on my experience with student problems. That was my psyche: I was very good at putting myself in those situations, understanding them and building from there. I find it easy to see things from people's perspectives, but very difficult to sympathise with what drives them. If you're driven by anxiety, or by the need for someone to tell you that you're doing a good job, or by social pressures, or anything other than just your own determination, then I find it really hard to relate to that. I don't know why.

*Ali: Something I teach in sales training is about personality types. If you're one type, you can sell really well to a couple of others, but there'll always be one or two you struggle with because you just can't see the world through their lens very easily. So, it's harder to present the information in a way that appeals to them directly.*

*Dom:* Yes, I think my biggest strength is also my biggest weakness. This is going to sound arrogant; but I've got a really short knowledge gap. If you tell me something once, I know it. I don't need things repeated, or context re-explained, or constant reaffirmation. My strength is in being able to connect the dots quickly. But my weakness is that I don't always recognise that other people aren't on the same page, or don't have the same recall. So they don't know why something has happened or why we should take a certain direction.

Take a creative meeting, for example. If we were pitching for a client, I'd say something like: 'We did this with Hungry House, we did this with Uber - these areas are easy for us, so the strategy needs to be X.' That would be my complete brief. I'd know exactly what I meant, because I had all the context in my head. But even people in the room who had worked on those projects couldn't always recall the intricacies of why it worked for those clients.

That's probably where my control-freak tendencies came in. Because I was running the project, running the campaign, running the creative. And I wasn't comfortable handing that over to someone who couldn't pull in all the cultural and societal context to create it at the same level because that felt like we were losing the creativity piece.

*Ali: I see this sometimes in founders where there's a real challenge because you have built up all this knowledge about your business and your subject and so you can make all the connections on a lot of things. It means you can almost jump into the middle of information, but trying to translate that into something that a whole team can follow is a real challenge.*

*Dom:* Yes, that's 100% my weakness. If someone doesn't understand what I'm saying, I know that's not a reflection on them - it's a reflection of how I communicated it.

I think that's where diversity in a leadership team really matters. You need different capabilities, and we definitely had that between us. But what we had in common was also important. We both had an almost blind delusion of confidence.

So, the things we had in common were powerful, and the things we had that were different were also powerful. We were very different individuals, driven by very different things. For example, Steve couldn't remember anyone's name, whereas I could recall every single person and conversation. I was basically the memory bank of the business. In pitches, Steve would handle the showmanship and the sale, and I'd bring the facts: 'We did this for X client, this was the result, this is the reach, these were the impressions'. Together it was convincing, because he brought the energy and I brought the data.

*Ali: Yes! I bet! I expect that with that pairing you could resonate with most people in the room.*

*Dom:* Exactly. Old white men preferred me – I wonder why... They just trusted me. They saw a younger version of themselves. Women loved Steven, as they still do today. So between us, we could cover most of the room.

* * *

# The Exit

## Preparation

*Ali: Did you always think you would exit one day?*

*Dom:* Yeah.

*Ali: That's interesting, particularly because the business was experimental to start with. Having always had the foresight that you would want to sell eventually is pretty impressive.*

*Dom:* We were both always in the mindset that we would use the business as our university and as our learning curve. So we would learn as much from it as we could. That philosophy stayed with us. We also always thought that we would be out of the business before we were 30, because we felt social media at the time was a young person's game. The world's obviously changed now, and to be in social media at 30 is absolutely fine and normal, but were 19 when we started, and it felt different.

We also raised money right from day one. We had investors very early, so we were in the world of equity, selling and returns from the start. And of course, once you've got investors, the conversation eventually becomes: how are they going to get their money back? That's when you think, 'Well, should we just sell the business?'. So, that plan was seeded very early. I don't think you can really raise much money from an investor without saying: 'At some point, we're going to sell'.

*Ali: How did you learn about investors, equity and share setups?*

*Dom:* Honestly, we didn't. One of our clients basically offered us money because we were doing a great job for them. From our perspective, that made sense: we could raise money from them - why not? It also secured their retainer for longer, so it was money plus long-term income, which is always a good place to be. Suddenly we were looking at it thinking, 'Oh my God, this is going to be a million pounds a year'.

But also personally, it meant security. If someone could give us money that secured our circumstances for the long term, then why wouldn't we do it? That was probably the driver. It was the point where we thought, 'Okay, what if we take this seriously, and we stop travelling the world, stop just having fun, and actually do this full-time?'.

*Ali: Did you get lawyers involved?*

*Dom:* They brought their lawyer in, a guy called Alex, who still works with both Steve and me today. Great guy. He basically said, 'I need some kind of business plan to attach to the documents'. So we went to Bill's, downstairs in Hammersmith near Lyric Square, and wrote a business plan with a red pen and a green pen. Green was money in, red was money out. We scribbled it out on a page, stamped 'business plan' on it, attached it to the investment documents - and that was our first business plan. One page, scribbled in pen.

*Ali: Amazing, I'd love to see it.*

*Dom:* I asked Alex if he still had it, and he looked but couldn't find it. The physical copy is gone, but I think there's a photo somewhere. Talking about shares and investments all became very normal to us after that. It's kind of wild when you think about the value of cash we were dealing with and the rooms we were suddenly in. The first picture we posted from an investment meeting was us in a room with a bunch of older men in suits. The first time you sit in that room you think, 'wow'. By the fifth time you know how it goes and it's normal.

Steve and I got comfortable very quickly. After the first couple of campaigns, you realise you can do what you want; you can play at that level. So, becoming accustomed to life and business in that way became second nature to us — probably because of our personalities. We were quite outgoing, quite likeable, or at least I like to think so. That made it easier.

From my perspective, one of the things I learned — and this is maybe different from Steve - is that I went to a school with no hierarchy. We called teachers by their first names. So I never had that "sir to pupil" mindset. I never saw adults as automatically right and me as automatically wrong. I was taught everyone is equal, regardless of age. From a young age we were encouraged to challenge teachers in healthy debate. So I was used to that.

Kids are often told that their parents and teachers are always right. From my perspective, I was never told that. I was never told to take things at face value. I was always taught to challenge, to think, to question. And that, for me, was a huge thing - something ingrained in me I never realised could be so powerful.

## Going Public

*Ali: How did the merger with Lumaland AG actually come about in the first place?*

*Dom:* Our chair, Georg Kofler, was our main backer. From day one, we shared the belief that social media was the future. Georg's first business, ProSieben, was a huge TV company in Europe, and his whole model was that if you owned both the content and the distribution, you'd win. We bought into that vision - that if you owned and operated businesses *and* the marketing channels for those businesses, you'd be successful.

So the logic of the Lumaland merger was this: it gave us access to the public markets so we could raise money, it gave us a portfolio of brands to work on; it gave us logistics, operations and warehousing in Germany and the Czech Republic, and it gave us a hedge against Brexit - because there was a real belief the UK economy was going to fall on its arse. What we brought to the table was the marketing and media expertise in the UK and US. They brought e-commerce operations. Together with money raised from the markets, the plan was to acquire businesses that we could scale through our platform.

The thinking was, 'We're tired of doing campaigns for Coca-Cola. Clients come and go. But if we had our own assets, that value creation would last forever'. And actually, that logic makes sense when you look at how the world's gone since. The first test of that strategy in the UK was with a small business called Adanola. Social Chain was their first investor; we took 30% of the company, and the plan was to hold and scale it. That deal ended up unwinding after Steve and I left, but if you look at Adanola now, the proof's in the pudding. If we'd found our MyProtein, our Gymshark, that model of owning and marketing our own businesses would have worked.

So, the deal completed in October 2019. We raised another 10% of share value through a roadshow, and by early 2020 we'd set out our agenda for what we were trying to build. And then - boom - COVID hit.

We had an events business in Germany called Shine Conventions, which ran Glowcon which is a beauty and influencer event. That was a fantastic business, doing about £15 million as part of the group. But in 2020, all of that revenue disappeared overnight. As a newly listed PLC in our first year, we suddenly lost £15 million of revenue. And in that position, you've only really got one option, which is to make your numbers.

So yes, we panicked. As a short-term PLC play, the only way to replace revenue fast is to buy it - distressed assets, poor purchases, whatever you can pick up. You buy the revenue; you hit the target; you account creatively if you need to. And that's what the group did. We layered on poor acquisitions rather than the right acquisitions, and the model fell apart.

*Ali: This sounds like a really stressful time?*

*Dom:* No, it wasn't. I'll tell you why. The key year was 2018. We consolidated the US business, the German business, the media business, and the events business into group valuations, which had to be approved by a judge in Berlin. Those valuations were based on our 2018 figures. So, hitting the 2018 numbers was everything. That was *the* threshold year.

The most stress I ever felt was on 3rd November 2018, pitching for a global project worth about £4 million. I knew how much it mattered. If we won it, we'd succeed. If we didn't, we might fail. Thankfully, we won. That was stress.

What changed the game was that project. It straddled 2018 and 2019, making both years look very healthy. I knew how important that revenue was, so I worked on Christmas Eve and Boxing Day in 2018 to make sure the project went live in December. I convinced the client to start on Boxing Day so the revenue would fall into 2018. If it hadn't, it would all have landed in 2019 and blown our numbers.

Even then, it was the tightest we ever came to not paying wages. We'd signed the contract, agreed everything, and they'd told us they'd pay in November. So we relaxed for the first couple of weeks. Then the last week of November came; I was in Paris with my girlfriend at the time - and the money still hadn't landed.

We ended up getting a signed PO from the client, sent it to our bank manager, and he released the funds by putting us about £300k into overdraft. It was Q4, ad spend was through the roof, Facebook credit limits were at £2 million, and cash was insanely tight. But we knew £4.5 million was coming down the line, so we could breathe. That was the closest we ever came to missing payroll. After that day, once the bank manager raised the funds, we were sorted. I never stressed about it again because the money came in around 2nd December and we could pay everything off.

Once that project was secured, signed, paid and delivered, I relaxed completely. That one campaign alone was about £4.5 million in revenue and around £3 million profit. When you add that on top of BAU (business as usual), we were in a fantastic position. By early 2019, when we approached Lumaland, we had our valuations agreed and rubber-stamped. They had a public market valuation; we had ours; and when you merged the two, the equity split was based on our contribution. That all came together around February or March 2019.

That 2018 Christmas into 2019 period was probably the biggest learning opportunity of my life. For me, it felt like my parting gift to the business. After that, in 2019, Steve and I weren't really involved day to day. We were focused on the deal, on selling the group, on group strategy and synergies.

On paper, the business looked really strong. I think we forecast £17 million revenue and about £4 million EBITDA that year. It was in good hands. But our focus was on the group, because that's where our interest lay once the merger was agreed.

And by then, it wasn't stressful at all. Our personal futures were secure. We were no longer responsible for payroll; the group was. Our remuneration was fixed based on our shares. They were in our bank accounts, and we could sell them if we wanted. So actually, it was the lowest stress I've ever felt, because you just stop caring.

## Negotiation

*Ali: What were you most grateful that you had in place when you were negotiating and going through this merger?*

*Dom:* The revenue, first and foremost, and the knowledge. Social Chain was always going to be a social-first business, so our value to the group was the revenue we could generate and the expertise we could bring to the board. But honestly, I don't think we were listened to as much as we could have been, because we were still young; we were about 26 or 27. At the group strategy level, we felt more like token appointments to the exec board.

With hindsight, if we'd led it, I think we'd have done it better. Georg, our German chair, was a big influence, but the Lumaland CEO remained in charge of the AG. That meant Steve and I weren't steering it in the way we might have.

*Ali: Is that why you didn't stay on in an advisory role like Steven did?*

*Dom:* I think we both knew our time was up. I spent a bit of time in Berlin handling the merger, getting to know people. But I remember going on holiday in February 2020 and just saying to myself: I'm done.

There was no motivation anymore. The work it would take to double our value felt pointless, because the influence I had was so nominal. Going back to the TikTok story, the way I could shape things now was so limited. It just felt pointless.

*Ali: You also said earlier that you felt more financially secure and that fear has been a big driver for you in the past. So it sounds like those two things coincided with when you felt like you weren't being heard?*

*Dom:* Exactly. That, and not enjoying the work anymore. Then COVID hit, and at first it brought the fear back – 'What if we lose everything?'. But once we realised the business would be fine, that was the final sign it was time to go. In a weird way, it made it exciting again for a short while, but by then the decision was clear.

*Ali: Did you make that decision together, or did one of you want to go first?*

*Dom:* I said I'd go first. But really, we sat there from March to May during COVID, when everyone else was at home, and me and Steve went into the office every day just talking through problems.

*Ali: Was it difficult to make the decision to leave?*

*Dom:* No. Because once you take the personal element out of it and you remove the reason you do the work, which is the people – it becomes logical. When the office was empty, or I was sitting at home by myself, I realised it was miserable. I stopped thinking about how much I loved seeing all the people on our team and going into the office. It was then easy to make a rational call. And that's what we did.

## Reflections

*Ali: A lot of times founders talk about feeling a sense of grief the next day. It sounds to me like you were already grieving it before you'd gone?*

*Dom:* Yeah, COVID killed it for me. It killed our relationship with the business. We were built on people, on community, on being together - and COVID ruined that. And honestly, looking around the corner, I always knew I wouldn't want to rebuild Social Chain in a post-COVID world. Whatever came after, it was going to be a slog, and I didn't want to do that. I wasn't going to try to run a business with 750 people coming out of a pandemic.

If there's a better time to jump ship, tell me. That was the best time. Especially with a people business. Even in the early days, having conversations about firing people was tough. So imagine redundancies, restructuring, changing the way people work. I was just staring into an abyss of problems. And for what? The return wasn't there.

That's the difference. You'll put in the effort if the return is there. If it's 'do this or fail', then fine, you'll do it. But this was different. I didn't *need* to do it. And that's a very different psyche.

*Ali: Yes, I can see that. If you can't see a return on that effort, then why would you?*

*Dom:* Why would I? When the other option is taking your money, sitting on a beach, and having a nice time with your family?

*Ali: Many of the readers of this book are founders that are interested in exiting their agency at some point. Whether that's in 6 months or in 6 years. They know they don't want to be in their agency forever, but they're also trying to translate where they are now into where they want to get to. What are the biggest lessons an agency founder should learn to help them secure their exit?*

*Dom:* I think the big balance is the role of the founder. Most agencies I've seen are founder-dependent - whether that's for delivery, strategy, sales, whatever. But the only way to create value in an agency is to make it *not* founder-dependent. Simple as that.

We always used to say that one day we'd just check out the back door because we wouldn't be needed anymore. And that's kind of what happened. After COVID, the business became structured differently. No one spoke to me. I couldn't just pick up the phone to a junior creative to chat about what they were seeing in the market, because who's going to answer a call from the COO on a random Tuesday? Everyone would assume it was bad news. So, those informal chats disappeared, and the business became rigidly structured.

I remember being wheeled into pitches - Ancestry was the big one. My total involvement was, 'Hi, I'm Dom. I'm the co-founder'. That was it. The team pitched; I just sat there. And that's basically what happened during COVID. The management team ran with their responsibilities, the structure solidified, and Steve and I were left trying to do all the group-level stuff.

It was infuriating. I remember May that year; the weather was amazing outside, and my week looked like this: Monday was the US board, Tuesday the UK board, Wednesday the German board, then Thursday and Friday were debriefs from all of them. Four or five board meetings in a week, plus all the issues being thrown around. Honestly, it was the worst week of my life. And then you try to get your actual work done in the scraps of time left.

So yeah, that's the key to an agency exit: make the founder redundant.

*Ali: How did you go about that?*

*Dom:* It was about the management team and replacing our capabilities. You've got to remove your ego a bit and admit there are better people than you for certain roles. Then, think about the role you *do* play.

For us, the timings mattered. We knew 2018 was our key year, 2019 was our transition into the group, and then COVID hit. By October 2019, we'd basically backfilled our roles. Six months later, we could look at it and say, 'We're not leading anymore'.

If COVID had happened at the start of 2019, it would've been very difficult. But the timing aligned. We'd already done the work to get the right team in place so that we weren't needed day to day, and that freed us up to focus on the group strategically.

In 2019 we brought in a client services director, Simon Whitaker from MediaCom. We had MDs formally appointed in the US and UK. Ops directors in both territories. A group CFO and an agency CFO. FDs in each area. A strategy director. A creative director. That was the mission for 2019: to build the structure so Steve and I weren't essential.

And then Bob's your uncle. A couple of months later, you're at Christmas, Q4 madness, still pretty hands-on. The new year starts well. I go on holiday in February for my sister-in-law's 30th. The day I get back we go into lockdown.

So in reality, I probably only worked January and February in 2020. After that, COVID hit, and by then the listing had already been done - it was 19th October 2019. So November, December, those four months were really the testing if the work we'd done in 2019 had actually set up the business to run without us. And it had.

*Ali: It can be hard to make yourself redundant if your identity is wrapped up in the business. How did you separate your ego from the task at hand?*

*Dom:* By that point we'd learned we weren't the best at everything. So I don't think I had an ego left. I'd learned quickly there are people better than you, and I was fine with that. I think your ego gets built in other ways. A lot of agencies need to walk into a room and feel like the most important person, because they don't get that validation anywhere else. I think I was lucky. From the early days, I'd already had millions of likes and comments on social media. It wasn't about me personally; it was about the brand, but that gave validation. Then, I started building my personal brand. You walk into rooms, and people know you. You win a couple of awards and suddenly you've got the prestige.

That meant I didn't need to exert ego in a room with my team. I didn't need to micro-manage people to prove myself. When your 'art' is recognised globally, and you've had that validation, you don't need to fight for it internally.

*Ali: I wonder if that felt different for you because even from early on, you were attracting brands to you?*

*Dom:* Yeah. The story. That was everything. And I think that's the key. Ego in an agency context often shows up as microaggressions - founders needing to dominate a room, sit back with all their awards behind them, play the narcissist. For some, the agency is their art, and they can't see beyond themselves. That's why they struggle to scale.

For me, I'd already had validation elsewhere. So I didn't need to behave like that.

* * *

## The Future

*Ali: What is the best piece of advice you would give to anyone who's running an agency?*

*Dom:* Make yourself redundant as quickly as you can. That is it. Figure out the piece where you add unique value and spend your time there. Turn everything else into a commodity and then work on making yourself redundant.

*Ali: Where do you think the future of agencies is heading with AI?*

*Dom:* I'm actually quite excited about the future of agencies. Let's talk about the UK, because that's where my experience is. Right now, businesses are on a mission to reduce headcount, reduce costs, and increase efficiency. One of the easiest ways to do that is to hire an agency rather than five people in-house. It gives them flexibility.

Agencies also have a role in keeping clients up to date with what's new and what's coming. So you've actually got a two-pronged market effect. On one side, service businesses become more efficient because of AI, so their costs come down. On the other, businesses don't want to take on headcount because they'd rather work with specialists who already have the expertise.

That's why I think it's a great time to start an agency. Yes, you're shouldering staff costs, but tech efficiency offsets that. And companies need agencies more than ever because the pace of change is so fast. In fact, I'd argue even accountancy firms are basically agencies if you strip it back.

The market is fragmenting. Companies want to keep their core teams lean. Culture gets harder to manage the bigger you get, so hiring five juniors in-house might upset the apple cart, whereas outsourcing keeps things stable. What I see is companies holding on to more senior staff, using AI to replace some junior work, and leaning more heavily on agencies for specialist expertise. Agencies will stomach the people problems like rising costs, national insurance, all that - and clients will just buy the output.

That's my theory of where it's going.

*Ali: What is your advice for agencies that are trying to adapt to AI quickly?*

*Dom:* My advice is to treat AI as the newest frontier. These frontiers come around every so often. The internet was one, the shift to digital was one, social media was another. You could even put smart devices in there. Each time, businesses either adapted, or they died. Look at Topshop versus Boohoo as an example. AI is the next one; and it's going to be bigger.

The key thing is that these cycles are getting shorter, and the impact is getting greater. AI will be more transformative than social media, and more transformative than the internet itself. So if you don't have a policy and a philosophy towards it, you're going to struggle.

The opportunity is credibility. Frontiers give you the chance to become an expert quickly. Back when we were 19, we could walk into a boardroom and say, 'We're experts in social media', and people listened because we had proof. No one else could point to having grown communities from zero to a million. Agencies live on case studies, and we already had one. That gave us instant trust.

It's the same with AI now. If you spend six months working hard, building something tangible, you can credibly say you're an expert, and people will believe you. That window doesn't stay open forever. My advice: don't wait, don't dabble. Go deep and go now.

*Ali: What's your advice for a founder who is burning out?*

*Dom:* Look at what you're doing. You're probably trying to do too much and take too much control.

My advice is to spend your time where it's most valuable, and trust other people. Look at the tasks you're doing that could be automated - and automate them! Look at the areas where you're holding on too tightly and give them to someone else.

I'm working with three founders right now who, in the last two weeks, have all found themselves doing customer service. Different sectors, not agencies, but it's the same principle. They're spending time on things that create more stress, not less. And your job as a founder isn't to do everything, unless it's literally just you.

So, think carefully about your resources, and how you build the right team around you. And then ask yourself some hard questions like:

- Are you charging too little?
- Are you doing too much work for the value you're generating?
- Do you have the wrong ICP?
- Or is your lifestyle simply not compatible with being a founder?

It's probably one of those.

*Ali: So, what's next for you?*

*Dom:* Events spun out of what we were doing at Social Chain. My view was always that if you're doing the marketing, you should also own equity in the business. If your CMO is sitting there as an investor, you're in a stronger position.

But the investment landscape is changing fast. Capital is more expensive, investments are being centralised and pushed into more liquid assets because of the global economic situation. Early-stage businesses are really struggling. If you're an early-stage founder asking me for £200–300k, my question now is: why wouldn't I just take that money and do it myself? The barrier to entry is coming down, and early-stage investment is pretty much fucked at the moment.

That's why I believe the venture studio model is the future. Instead of just investing in other people's companies, we're looking at how to compete by starting and launching our own businesses. That's where my focus is.

## Finding Dominic McGregor

You can find Dom on Instagram @dpjmcgregor and Linkedin: linkedin.com/in/dpjmcgregor/

* * *



* * *

# Exit Story Takeaways

**1. Redundancy creates value**

Dom's number one lesson is that the fastest way to add value is to make yourself redundant. Buyers don't want a founder-shaped hole in the organisation chart because that brings risk. Instead, they want to see teams, structures, and systems that run smoothly without you.

**2. Your product isn't enough**

Social Chain began with disruptive assets (those huge student audiences!). That got attention, but it wasn't enough to scale without taking on senior hires. Agencies that last are built on more than founder ability. To grow into something sale-ready, you need a structure in place: senior hires, strong operations, and proper financial control.

**3. The power of an enemy**

Dom and Steven united their team against a common enemy: old-school advertising that didn't have the reach of social media. This clear position attracted talent and clients to Social Chain, because they knew what it stood for - and against.

**4. Don't miss the frontier**

Dom and Steven rode the early wave of social media perfectly. Years later, Dom spotted TikTok before most - but the agency had become too rigid to pivot. Value appears when you act on new frontiers *before* the herd moves: whether that's social in 2013, or AI today.

**5. Pressure creates diamonds**

That terrifying £4 million global pitch ultimately locked in Social Chain's valuation. So often, it's the scary moments that make or break business value. Once the pressure had receded, Dom's motivation and love for the business dropped too.

# IV

# Change Is The Only Constant

# 9

# The Unscheduled Dismount

Founders and horse riders have a lot in common. Both the founders and horse riders work with beasts much larger than themselves, often enjoy wonderful relationships with them, but also frequently get reminded they are very much unable to control the other entity. Just as things are going smoothly, there's a humongous buck, a kick or an accidental headbutt. We dust ourselves off, ready to go again.

I started riding when I was about 3. The moment I found horses I 'got the bug' and have never shut up about them since. It'll be no surprise to my friends and family that they've shown up in this book somewhere. It's a wonder I get invited anywhere, really.

A dismount is the moment you collect your reins up, hold the horse still and swing your leg to get off quietly. An unscheduled dismount is an expression used by riders as they confide in each other with love and laughter. It is code for 'I fell off' or perhaps 'I had to jump off before I crash landed'. It's mainly used in situations where the fall was disappointing, but you were uninjured, a little bruised emotionally, but probably got back on again intending to try again another day. Occasionally it's used in more serious falls, but only once you're ready to talk about it and try to laugh off the broken ankle you have sustained while playing with your 500 kg fire-breathing dragon.

I am so grateful for being able to include Jack Porter-Smith and Jon Payne's stories. Both made an unscheduled dismount, but for very different reasons and in very different ways. In Jack's story, we'll learn why planning for an exit is an insurance policy. He never wanted to leave, but thank goodness he had prepared his agency so that he could. In Jon's story we'll hear about burnout, and how, despite a lack of preparation, Jon landed on his feet, bowed to the crowd and walked out of the arena ready to ride again next week. It's one of the most creative deals I have come across.

# 10

# Let Go Of Your Lego

*"You're only as good as you are to your team.*
*As soon as you're a hypocrite, they're gone and you're done."*
*– Jack Porter-Smith*

**Entrepreneur:** Jack Porter-Smith
**Exit Type:** Shares sold to his co-founder
**Exited Agency:** Utopiads
**Time to Exit:** 11 years
**Exit Value:** Undisclosed
**Profit:** £2million Net
**Employees at Exit:** 25
**Purchaser:** Jack's co-founders at WSI

Jack, AKA 'Snacky', recently exited the transatlantic agency he co-founded and lovingly nurtured for 11 years. I found myself in awe of his raw honesty and his resilience through a time that no one would wish on their worst enemy.

Jack's story is unusual. He didn't want to leave his agency, nor was he forced to by his board, - in fact, they were always incredibly supportive of him throughout his exit story. He'd turned down dozens of unsolicited offers for the agency over the years, and was so committed he did his agency planning not in years, but decades. In Jack's beautifully poignant resignation letter, he wrote of his love both for, and from, his team. They loved him, and he didn't want to leave. So how did this eight-figure agency leader go from being an all-in 'lifer' to walking away?

My conversation with Jack took place just six months after his 'emergency exit'. He shared with me that his focus was on simply 'staying alive'. His charm, sense of humour, and wonderful Scottish accent made for an engaging and enjoyable conversation. But our fun was interspersed with difficult moments, sadness and a clear sense of grief for the agency he had loved so much.

Jack started the agency when he was just 23. Incredibly, he had the foresight from day one to build an agency that could be exited, even though it was something he never thought he'd want (or need) to do. In the following pages, you'll come to understand why this honest interview was both fun and heartbreaking. Through Jack's words, we'll explore how he came to exit and how he had prepared his agency for an eventuality he never thought would come true.

* * *

## The Entrepreneur

## Origins

*Ali: To get us started, tell us how your career began.*

*Jack:* I think the story began at school. I was bad at school - like really bad. I was always in detention. I got kicked off almost all of my courses. My dad established fairly early on that money incentivised me. So, he made a system where it was something like £100 for an A, £50 for a B - whatever it was. With this in place, I took all five classes that I could in my final year. By Christmas, I'd been kicked off three of them.

So, a couple of weeks after turning 16, I left school and got a job as pretty much a tea boy at a local family-run agency. On my first day, I was like: 'What is a PPC?', 'What is an SEO?'. I really didn't know; I was just out of school. I had always wanted to join the police, and so I had thought that the agency role would be a stop gap until I turned 18. So I waited until I could apply to the police and went through all the fitness tests, the exams, and all that stuff. I made it through all of that and to the final interview with the big boss, which is when they declined me due to 'a lack of life experience'. I felt that if they were going to do that, why even let an 18-year-old apply? But if you get to the final interview, then you automatically get into the Special Constables. You have all the same equipment, powers, and training, but it's voluntary and you have to go out with a full-time cop. I did that for six or seven years while also climbing the ranks in the digital marketing world.

In that first agency job, I was mostly running reports and making tea, but of the exposure to digital marketing I had, PPC was the most interesting to me by far. So I moved into a PPC role and hopped jobs every 18 months or so when I outgrew my employer.

Having been declined by the police was a blessing in disguise because I realised it was a horrible job. Even in my limited exposure to that world, there were some things that made me think, 'I don't know that I would want to do this for the rest of my life' - and on a very regular basis. Hats off to those who do it, but it was dangerous, and by that time, I was already earning more money in marketing than I would have in the police. Money isn't everything, but when you're hyper-independent and in your late teens or early 20s, you want your first flat, your first car, and you want to start investing in your relationship (I met my wife at 20).

So, I took the marketing route more seriously. I went through a few more jobs and then, at 21, I was 5 years in and working at a great agency. It was called Peach Digital in Glasgow and was owned by a really cool guy called Mike Rose. For some bizarre reason, he made me Head of Marketing almost straight away, even though I was only 21. I knew nothing about leadership. I was good with clients and I was great with the product, so he took a chance on me. I told him I was really happy there, and that I didn't think I'd ever leave unless it was to do my own thing - and that's ultimately what happened when I was 23.

*Ali: I feel you could be downplaying your skills a bit when you say you don't know why he would make you the head of marketing. You must have* shown *him some skills that he was excited about. How and why did you start an agency?*

*Jack:* I think many people tell you they're accidental founders. I see that all the time, and so must you. It was never on my radar, but three years into my career, I started posting on a forum. It was run by Google and focused on Google Ads. I posted to help other people and because I was bored with my day job. I got my work done and didn't have anything else to do, so I thought I might as well learn because teaching is the best way to learn, right?

On this forum, you'd find really weird technical problems. I'd have to go away, figure it out, and then post the answer. A couple of years into that, Google called me and said, ‘Hey, do you want to be a Top Contributor?’ - which was basically like becoming the grand wizard of the forum. The cool thing was that you got a bunch of perks! Once or twice a year, Google flew the Top Contributors to one of their cool HQs for a few days of socialising, meeting product managers, and testing new things before they were released to the public. So I became a bit of a famous ‘grand wizard’ within PPC, which, nearly 20 years ago, was an especially small circle.

I really love this part of my story because it wasn’t planned. I didn’t even know the programme existed, and I wasn’t trying to achieve anything. It just happened. I got rewarded for helping people online every day. I could never have realised the doors that would open for me, the acclaim it would get me and the deals I would win. I think that’s the best story, and that’s something I always told employees about when they started with us. I said to them, ‘If you want to be really good, help other people. Go on the forums, Reddit, the Google Ads forum, whatever it is. Look at people’s problems and help them. I can teach you, you can go to workshops, and you can read books, but it’s not the same thing’. It was helping people that accidentally got me what I got. And I think that’s probably the coolest part.

That Top Contributor attention led to my co-founder in Toronto discovering me. One day when I was working at Peach Digital, I got an email connecting me to the CEO of WSI, which is a big franchisor of a thousand digital marketing agencies. And they were like, ‘Hey, we have a bunch of agencies, but some of them are not fully PPC capable. Do you want to come and help?’. My idea was that I’d just fly around the world training all their agencies to do PPC better. I still wasn’t thinking that it would lead to starting an agency. They said, ‘We’ve got a better idea. Why don’t we just set up a PPC agency together and you can help them deliver?’ and so it was born. That was my weird, unplanned, 7 year journey to starting the agency.

*Ali: What skills do you have that made you right for leading an agency?*

*Jack:* Like many agency founders, I was very good at my trade - PPC. This is funny because earlier you said that I was downplaying why they would have made me Head of Marketing at Peach, but I think it's just an observational fact. Half of the reason I succeeded was that I was a Brit in North America. Honestly, you've probably seen it yourself - there is an effect of the accent and as soon as you tell anyone you're from West Scotland, they'll say, 'Oh, I'm a fifth Irish and quarter Scottish.' and it opens so many bonding conversations.

I think my most useful skills were my deep product expertise and my ability to get along with people. We launched at a big conference with 500 other agencies, and straight away we could connect on a human level. The business has always come second to the human connection for me.

Ultimately, I was very good at PPC. And I deliberately use the past tense on that because the longer you run an agency, the less of the trade bit you do. I would be hopeless now. You wouldn't let me anywhere near an account because I'm just too out of date. But I was good at my trade, and that was the crux of it.

## Mindset

*Ali: What was your mindset while you were building Utopiads?*

*Jack:* I've enjoyed meeting you as a good human, and someone who gets things. But early on, I didn't want to get out there and meet people - that's something I've developed later on. In those very early days, I just wanted to make money. That was my primary motivator for accepting the deal, going to Canada, and being brave. So, networking was really something I had to do, and I could naturally do it. I know it sounds really cynical looking back, but it's my honest reflection. It wasn't that I was an extreme extrovert and wanted to grow my network. I think that maturity came eight or nine years into it.

I found I wanted to bond with people on a human level. Several years in, I was at a Google meeting where I was on the Agency Executive Council. The night before, I thought I'd take some clients out for dinner, and I invited some prospective clients. The bill was a good few thousand - you know what it's like with 20-30 digital marketing people blowing off steam. At the end, one guy called Jason said, 'I don't really know why you invited me or why you're being so generous'. And I was like, 'Because I just want to bond'. And he said, 'Why aren't you asking me for anything?'. He really didn't understand what I was doing, but in my mind I was just bonding. They accepted me as the human that I was, and the business took care of itself after that.

*Ali: To go to Toronto and start a new business at 23 is pretty brave. Were you scared?*

*Jack:* Do you know that's the other ridiculous thing? Even though I was flying around for business meetings, I wasn't scared at all. We had just bought a house. It was a stretch purchase, and Lisa's dad was over visiting, and he asked what I was going to do next, and I said, 'Oh, I'm thinking about starting a business'. He was like, 'Oh, in a few years, right? Once things are settled?'. And I was like, 'No, this week!'.

The risk just never bothered me - I hope that was more self-belief than cockiness. But my position was good because I was doing a co-founder joint venture, and they had approached me to run it, so part of the deal was that they would give me an office and the resources I needed. They even guaranteed my salary for the first 6 months. It was a fairly lucky position to be in compared to many other founders who probably don't even pay themselves for the first year.

That salary was also a 50% increase on what I was on at Peach. So I was like, well, I'm guaranteed a much higher wage for 6 months, and if it fails, I'm quite employable if I have to come home with my tail between my legs. So quite honestly, I didn't have any fear whatsoever. I was also flown to Paris for the first meeting, Toronto for the second. I had my eyes wide open and couldn't believe it! I would have said yes to anything.

If I were starting an agency now, knowing everything I know, I'd be terrified. But I had that blissful youthful naivety, and blissful ignorance. I've thought about this a lot, and I am kind of mad that it took my innocence away from me. You know there are a few moments in everyone's mind where you look back and say, 'I lost 20% of my innocence that day'.

I was thrown into a whole new world at 23 with big conferences on a different continent. You can say the wrong thing completely inadvertently. You can get dragged into situations you didn't really want to be in or shouldn't have been in. So, I think that was the trade-off. It robbed quite a lot of that from me. But the upside is that until I lost my naivety and innocence, I wasn't scared of anything and had total belief that I would be a success - which was ultimately because I was very good at my job.

*Ali: Do you have any regrets?*

*Jack:* No, I mean, there are a couple of micro actions or behaviours I wish I hadn't engaged in or hadn't got carried away with, and times I wish I hadn't been led astray. But for the overall opportunity, how could you ask for it to be changed when it was so wonderful and organic? It just happened. I think most people never get an opportunity like that. I don't know that I would change things, but it came at a price, or in fact, various prices.

*Ali: What would you say to someone starting an agency?*

*Jack:* It'll be harder than you think, and you won't make as much money as you think.

When I was flying back from the negotiation in Toronto, I remember sitting at the gate with an A4 pad. I was stupid enough that I was writing out how many clients we'd get and the pricing I would do, and using it to work out how quickly I could become a millionaire.

I think that was over ambition of youth and not realising what the true value of building a meaningful agency would be, which was completely different. It's really easy to say now that my advice would be to start it for the right reasons, because if you go into it really just out of hunger it will become difficult. I don't think there's anything wrong with starting a company to make money, but I don't think that can sustain you through the decades and get you through tough times. And the reality is most people don't really achieve their monetary dreams. So try to have something else that drives you.

But maybe it's a fool's errand trying to convince someone of that. Maybe that's just something you have to learn from being out there and stubbing your toes.

Beyond that, I would tell them to help people. Just help as many people as you can without any expectations and leave it all up to karma and the bank of goodwill.

* * *

## Building The Agency

## Development

*Ali: Tell us about Utopiads and how it developed over time.*

*Jack:* It doesn't matter what type of business you start; it will be completely different in a decade. The business you design on a piece of paper will transform, and it will be dragged and stretched.

In the beginning, we were a production centre. We went into a network with hundreds of other agencies that had great in-house dev, SEO, and whatever else, but they did not have a strong PPC offering. So we filled that gap, partnered with them, and split the revenue. It was awesome because once I'd earned their trust, they would bring prospects to us. It was kind of like shooting fish in a barrel. But we still had to deliver, because if you mess up the opportunity, then you're going to lose the partner and maybe all 10 of the clients that they brought with them.

So that's what we were in the beginning. Our core function of paid media advertising never really changed, but we added some ancillary services and crucial sister services. By the time I left, attribution was a full-blown part of our business, whereas in the beginning it was something for the client to deal with. I think that's a journey many agencies have been through where they end up taking ownership of more of the road to success, instead of letting other people fail to solve it. Because if other stuff fails, then the advertising fails too.

You asked me about Utopiads' USPs and setup - I think most agencies would all say similar things. You know, what they do, their accreditations, certifications, that they're a Google Premier Partner, blah blah blah. But our DNA was to help people. I read *Traction,* and it helped me define my purpose and my company's purpose, which was to help people - so that became our whole thing. Whether it was events, books, or the way we did consultations - everything we did was about helping people. That applied to our staff too. I did this whole employee welfare review and completely reimagined the best way to look after my people. That's what drove me every day. I started the agency hungry and wanting to make loads of money, but in the end it was about being as useful as possible to as many people as possible. I think that really shone through.

## Growth

*Ali: What did new business look like at your agency?*

*Jack:* The agency changed by the end of my journey because I rebranded it and I changed where we got our new business.

We started as 'WSI Paid Search', which was the least imaginative name on the planet. It was just what we quickly came up with while we were in the boardroom signing the contract. It was a name for a production house, so it didn't need to be sexy to the outside world. But after about seven years, I'd got bored, and as wonderful as serving these other agencies was, our biggest problem was that we were not in control of our own destiny. We didn't know how many leads we were going to get, and we had no control over our pipeline. It wasn't just the client volume and frequency, but also the type of clients. One client might be a lawn mowing company for £750 a month, and then the next would be a multinational bank for 50 grand a month. There was no targeting or choice for us, and I really didn't like that. When you're trying to develop business plans, grow, and feed your team, it's exceedingly difficult when you're just a passenger.

So, I took the agency public. We came out from behind the curtain, rebranded, and ended up on this crazy public speaking tour of the Americas with Google. By the end, that was our primary identity. But we never abandoned our partners. It was more like 'Hey, we're going to go out and find ourselves in the outside world, and see what's really going on instead of hiding behind you, and then when we find what works, we'll bring it back to you'.

I discovered I was good at using public speaking to grow my agency. I did that for about a year, and a bunch of partners in our ecosystem heard about it. I wrote a book about it and at the annual conference, 400 of us got together, and I gave them a keynote to show them how I was doing it so they could do it too. We always brought the value back into the family, even though we were kind of flying on our own at that point.

Ultimately, our USP was education first. Many people could say that if they throw up an occasional LinkedIn post or something, but we had a track record of published books, countless events, and the evidence. That drove us forward both internally and externally. I think that's why our acquisition and retention were so successful. We didn't really put ourselves first very often.

*Ali: Yes! Genuinely trying to share information and to help educate brings in huge rewards. This is something I have always enjoyed when I've been building out sales teams. We can start with helping people as the goal, and then the sales flow after that.*

*Jack:* Yeah! And you can see the same thing at the beginning of my career with the forums. If you help people, good stuff happens. Obviously, as an agency owner, that becomes a bit more calculated - like we're going to help people, but those people will be 300 CMOs from Toronto. Some of them might want to hire us afterwards, and that's great. It was really important to me that there were no hard pitches, and that there were no credit card machines at the door of our events. Everyone always got things to take away, and they felt like they were at university for half a day and not at a pitch-fest.

It's funny actually; we did our quarterly pulse from the EOS system of *Traction*, where we gave each other feedback. My number one employee, who basically ran the agency, gave me a pro and a con. His con was that I'd stopped learning, and it really stung. It took me a minute to figure out why - it hurt because he was right. He had observed that I was the king of my ant colony and cruising. I was having fun and not taking any courses or reading enough books. Because of his feedback, I went on a sales course, and it was incredible. It helped me realise that in sales you have to manage your boundaries and control the conversations. I was in class two hours a week for a year, which satisfied my number one employee that I had resumed learning too.

*Ali: Did you have public speaking training?*

*Jack:* When we launched, I was thrown into the big annual conference of agency owners, and I did the worst keynote you can imagine. It was so bad I phoned my dad afterwards and cried. I just wanted to go home and forget the whole Canadian adventure. About four or five years later, we were doing well with Google, and someone from their 'black ops' style team called me and said, 'We've been tracking you guys. We want to bring you into this top 1% club'. And I was like, 'Cool. What does that mean?'. And they said, 'Well, we help you grow your agency. Whatever it takes'.

In the beginning, it was all very production focused and would be things like using their resources to build out our clients' work in five different languages. Later, we needed training, and so they would take my team down to their big office in Toronto.

One day I was at head office, and they had a public speaking workshop on. I'd had limited public speaking exposure at that point. I'd trained rooms of about 30, and I'd done some webinars here and there. So I saw this workshop and popped my head through the door. I thought,

'That looks cool,' and ended up taking part in the class for the whole day. I learned a lot. There were exercises, practice presentations, silly games, and some peer feedback. I was shocked at the end of the class when they said I'd got top of the class! I didn't even know it was being graded.

It was a surprise, but it was also a major confidence boost. Afterwards, I went to the head of the Google black ops team, and I said, 'I think I'm quite good at public speaking. Can we use that?'. She got a budget to run their first pilot, which we used on an event in downtown Toronto. She said, 'If you fill this event and you bring new revenue to Google, we might be on to something here'.

That's how I ended up holding my first event. It was 2018, and I was 5 years in. We had the YouTube room, which had a capacity of 55, and we packed it out - there wasn't a single seat spare. It was horrendous compared to what I could do now, but it worked and we got a client spending a million dollars a year on ads. They were new to Google and new to us. So straight out of the gate, it more than paid for itself and we had our proof of concept. After a few weeks, we met with the Google black ops team, and they said, 'Spin a globe. Pick anywhere you want to go, as many times as you want. Let's go'. And that was it.

We went all over the world, and they held us accountable after every event. Some of them were pretty disastrous, but we learned from those. After a year or two, we'd worked out the best cities for us. For example, we packed our Chicago event every time we went. We could fill it with 300-400 people, even if we went three times in the same year. You would think going back to the same city with the same event would stop working, but it worked really well for us. We found that if there were people in the room who didn't book a consultation the first time, the second time they would convert - and we won a bunch of work like that.

I wrote a book about my public speaking experience, and in it I try to convey that my story is my story; yours can be yours. I know not everyone's going to get a tour of the Americas with Google.

*(Ali: Jack's book is called 'Sixty Seconds of Glory: Selling From The Stage For Wildly Predictable Agency Growth' and is available on Amazon.)*

## Building Your Team

*Ali: What are your thoughts on teams and management?*

*Jack:* You're only as good as you are to your team. As soon as you're a hypocrite, they're gone and you're done.

So, like in the example earlier, if I'm driving people to learn and pestering them to use their education budget, then I can't be a hypocrite. If you can't take feedback back from your team, you've already lost. It's something that takes a bit of learning because it's not nice being criticised upwards - you feel a bit embarrassed.

I have an example from just before COVID hit in February 2020. My team member Lennena texted me saying, 'Hey, are you worried about this COVID-19 thing?' and I completely brushed it off. I was like, 'Nah, we're fine. I don't see how some disease spreading in Asia is going to affect our agency in Canada'. Then, within two weeks of that text, the whole world melted down, and I felt really stupid. I don't know why I didn't take her warning seriously, or see it coming myself. When you make a mistake as a leader, it's a chance to learn. Maybe I was busy, maybe my head was in a different space that day when the text arrived, but I should have considered it deeper, right? I should have got on a call with her and said, 'Tell me exactly what you're thinking. Why are you asking me this? What are you worried about?'. And instead, I just brushed it off because I thought I had to be the know-it-all confident leader. But leadership is all about listening and not arrogantly dismissing things.

I think it's also about learning to control your ego. When I was 23, I was a hotshot who was great at what I did. That meant I was welcomed into my new world with open arms. Which can inflate your ego, and if you don't control that, it will seriously damage your relationship with your team. That said, to some extent I think we all should have an ego - because that's really just self-belief. But it's how you show it and how you manage it. I think that COVID text is an example where I still didn't have it fully in check.

I think when you drop your guard, and stop being the 'Charge forward no matter what' type leader, your team sees it and it can be a little unsettling at first, but then they adapt. They realise that you're letting them be part of the solution-making team, which is better than always doing the problem solving yourself. At one point, we were losing like 35 grand a month. It was a first for us. We'd never lost money before, and it was quite an alarming amount of cash. I alluded to it with the team, but I never told them about it outright. I started issuing edicts like, 'We must double down here', 'You rattle that bush', 'You see what comes out of that tree', 'You stop losing clients'. We turned it around in a few months, and we were fine. But at the end of the year, I was giving my team 360 appraisals of the year. My team member Sanju bollocked me - and fairly. She said, 'We had no idea things were that bad. You should have told us so we could be part of the solution instead of trying to take it all on your own shoulders'.

They taught me so much. Everything I'm good at and everything I know now is because of them. They're brilliant.

* * *

# The Exit

## Preparation

*Ali: You never wanted to exit. So how did you come to do so?*

*Jack:* My whole everything sank once I realised you were pivoting us to this. I forgot we're here to talk about agency exits. It's not all rainbows and happy endings. At the end of my resignation letter, I wrote, 'I leave with a heavy but fulfilled heart,' and that's the best way I can put it.

I just didn't want to do it. I'd turned down multiple unsolicited offers, and naively I thought I would be there forever. I always talked to my team in decades. I think I've painted a positive picture of our story at the agency, because that's true. But don't get me wrong, we also had tough quarters and tough years like anyone else. But I always said to them, 'I couldn't care less. I don't mind a poor quarter, or even a poor year or two, because if we win seven or eight years out of the decade, then we're good. If we keep doing that decade after decade, we'll be fine'. I had visions of going non-exec in the future when I felt like it. I thought that perhaps in 10 years I might become a bit less hands-on and perhaps stay on as chairman. But I was supposed to be there forever.

*Ali: For the benefit of our readers, what changed?*

*Jack:* The simple answer is 'health'. Specifically, it was because of Crohn's disease. It's been 3 months, and I'm standing now, but a few months ago I was very unwell. My illness had been building for over 2 years, and it got to a point of near death, really.

I first realised something was wrong in 2019 when we were doing a Google event in New York. I got a call at 7am, 'We need to move everyone to a different building three blocks away'. It was January in

New York, so it was freezing and dark. We had to shift the entire event across the city because there was a security issue. So, it was a really stressful morning. While I was getting ready for the event, I had to go to the bathroom, and it was just pure blood in the toilet. I think that's the greatest possible demonstration that your mental and physical health are interlinked. No one gets Crohn's like that overnight. It builds up and you could have it for years without knowing you've got it. But it's exacerbated by stress, and this moment was a clear demonstration of that.

I did the event, and then I went home and got a diagnosis. Other than this, I was having the time of my life. We were flying, and I was headlining a lot of events. It was great, but it was still stressful. Evidently, I was stressed or I wouldn't have been bleeding out my ass. So, I've learned to understand that I should have listened to my body and stopped back then when I got diagnosed.

I was offered surgery there and then, but I kept declining it. They gave me steroids to get me through a bad few months. I had events I wanted to do, and I was busy. So for years I just kept pushing my surgery and fobbing off my team of medics.

In 2023, four years post-diagnosis, I was a mess. I was doing my best, but I wasn't the Jack everyone knew. During our off-site planning meetings, I would end up lying on a couch because I was in so much pain. But the meetings were important to me, and we had to get through them. When I look back, I can see that my abilities declined as my health did, but I never wanted to let go because I was having too much fun. I was on a roll, and things were going well. There was adrenaline in it. And maybe it's not until you stop and take a minute that you realise how much pain you're in. There's quite a lot of evidence that a certain number of people don't know they've been stabbed or lost a leg because of the adrenaline taking over. And I see it as a really long five-year version of that. I was having so much fun that I had no idea how much damage I was doing to my body.

In March 2024, I started being more open with my board and my team. In a loving way, they said, 'You need to take as long as you want. Come back however and whenever you want, but look after yourself. You've given everything you've got'. So everyone piled in and took over for me. People were promoted to temporary acting positions. Silent board members became active board members. We made changes, and I rested. But I didn't get any better.

I was hoping it'd be a couple of months and then I'd come back right as rain. But actually, I got worse throughout the year. I was hospitalised within a month of starting my health break. I avoided surgery at the time, but people kept texting me. It was all well-intended, but they were messaging, 'How are you doing?', 'Any better yet?', 'When are you coming back?', 'What role are you going to come back in?'. Imagine having a team of 25, plus 50+ active partners, plus other stakeholders checking in on you. And that's just your work crowd! Even at home, I started yelling at my mum, 'Stop asking how I am. I'll tell you when I feel better. I don't need to tell you I feel shit every day!'. Everyone checking in made me feel like I couldn't relax, and you can't heal if you're not relaxed and resting. That was coupled with the added stress that I was still getting worse, not better.

Toward the end of the year, I had an honest conversation with my board and my co-founder and I said, 'I'm very unwell. I have absolutely no way of knowing if and when I'm going to be better'. People needed answers from me, and I couldn't give them any. I could have an acting managing director for 6 months, maybe 12. But we couldn't do that for years. I was a very active managing director at the time. So, there were all kinds of decisions that had to be made so that the business could move forward. I was holding everyone and everything up.

It was the best part of a year before I left. I felt uncomfortable about the decision, and also about my still being an active shareholder. I was getting dividends and payouts and doing nothing for them. It didn't sit right with me. I was also concerned that if they had to replace me, it'd probably take three or four people because, like every founder, I did a lot of things. So I would think, 'What if they just gave 10% shares to four really shit-hot up-and-comers as part of their packages?'. I knew they could do that with my shares. So there were a few different things that led to the decision, but overall I just felt it was the right thing to do.

Within days of deciding, my health became the worst it had ever been. My life was in real danger. So in January 2025, I had several emergency surgeries. It shows I did the right thing, and that I made the right call. I had to take as much time as I needed to look after myself, and that's what I've done. So here I am now, 6 months post-exit and a few months post-surgery.

*Ali: When I first met Jack, we talked about his reasons for exit and I remember feeling a pang of horror as he described to me just how much danger he had been in during those surgeries. He shared how he had been instructed to record a video for his young son, in case he didn't wake up from one of the procedures. During both of our meetings, there was clear tension in Jack. He was torn between the need to recover and the desire to keep pushing on. Mostly, it was clear that his love for his wife and son overrode everything else and was what kept him wanting to spend time healing.*

## Negotiation

*Ali: How did you negotiate a deal you never wanted?*

*Jack:* It was a strange one. Neither of us wanted to be in this situation, and now we were forced to have these conversations. My co-founder didn't want this either. They were the silent one. I was the active one. I felt bad because I burdened them with my shares, and as a result, my problems. They carry on. No one person is bigger than a business, even me, right? You rehire and you move on. But it was strange, and I think both of us had the well-being of the team, our clients, and our partners at the front of our minds.

I know it sounds a bit bigheaded, but I've done alright. I've had more rewards than I could have imagined in my 35 years so far. So, the really easy part for me is that I wasn't bothered about the money. I just wanted to solve the problem.

Everything you do should be fair and equitable as far as it's reasonably possible. But the thing is, we always had the agency exit ready. That's something my co-founder Dan always taught me. Whether you want to sell or not, have it exit-ready. So that's how we approached things like client risk profiles, cash reserves, our growth trajectory, and our client contracts.

During those conversations, we'd talked about what an exit would look like and what it would be worth over the years. We weren't planning to do anything about it, but we had the conversations. So when it came to this negotiation, we were already philosophically on the same page. There wasn't any back and forth. It was more, 'So what's a fair price for my shares?', 'Okay, is that okay with you?', 'Yeah, it's okay with me'.

There was no bullying or throwing numbers at each other, no screaming or demanding. It was me that put forward the offer. I said, 'Look, I'm not trying to take the piss here. I just think this is a fair exchange, and it will free the agency up to move forward and grow. It gave my family an extra bump so I could afford not to work for 3 years'. So it was easy and quick.

*Ali: Did you have lawyers involved?*

*Jack:* Hilariously, we didn't get lawyers involved until it turned out that our original contract was completely void. When we tried to process the sale of my shares, we realised our initial agreement was full of holes. So they couldn't transfer my shares to my co-founder until I actually had them. It's funny because in some ways, I never actually owned anything. At the time we'd been so focused on launching an agency that we hadn't formally sorted our shareholder agreements. We had just trusted each other, and in the 11 years that followed, it was never an issue. So the lawyers helped us with a one-page addendum sending my shares to him, and that was it.

## Reflections

*Ali: What were you most grateful to have prepared for when it came to your exit?*

*Jack:* I always focused on having a healthy team and a healthy business. I never really bothered about paperwork. Most people don't believe me, but I have never logged into the agency bank account or raised an invoice. Not once. All things money, finance, documentation - I don't have any interest in them, so I pay little attention to them. So there we are.

*Ali: Part of what I'm trying to do with this book is to help agency owners build an exit-worthy business - whether that's for an exit that's in a couple of years, or further away. What had you put in place that made your exit easier? What are you glad you did?*

*Jack:* My co-founder Dan's advice was that a healthy agency is one that's ready to exit. So, I always looked for what was unhealthy and what was a risk. Then I did what I could about the threats because every weakness and threat you remove makes you more attractive to a buyer.

Not many agencies could be bought and successfully transitioned without a great team. Even if the new owner fires half of them, the people are a huge part of an agency - even in this AI world.

The other thing for me was diversity in new business. We had new business coming out of our ears. Sometimes the only reason an agency might get bought is its pipeline, its brand and its consistent ability to generate leads.

You can talk about systems, but they will rarely mesh with the acquirer. Every acquirer will have their own way of doing things. So while systems are important, they're buying the people, whichever way you want to look at it. The people could be the clients, the staff, the lead sources...

I say this, but it's from a man who has so much wisdom that he's accidentally sold one agency. I'm not an expert on this.

*Ali: Well, I think having an exit-ready agency is not a given. I meet a lot of agencies that have a pair of co-founders, sometimes even three or four. They couldn't exit because if one of them needed to sell their shares, the thing couldn't quite survive without them.*

*Jack:* A fundamental answer to that is the company has to be cash-rich. The founder has to be cash rich, and the company has to be cash rich; otherwise, no one's sending each other millions of dollars. If you have four co-founders who have been bleeding the company dry and mismanaging it, it doesn't have any cash reserves. If each of them is skint and buried in credit card debt, that situation will never end well.

My co-founder and I never talked about net worth with each other, not once in 11 years, but I believe he's extremely successful and sensible. We always put 30% of the profit into reserves. So even if we were way above our five-month operating cost minimum, that was still something we did. Sometimes we used our surpluses for strategic investments, or perhaps even high-risk growth opportunities that we wouldn't necessarily do out of cash flow. But ultimately, it was being so strong cash-wise that made the whole thing mechanically extremely easy. No one had to take out finance.

I also liked the EOS from the book *Traction*. I credit so much of our story to that book. I'm the absolute number one fan of Gino Wickman. He actually endorsed my upcoming book. But the point is, if you just read *Traction* and implement EOS, you're probably going to have a healthy-ish business and therefore a business you can probably sell if you want to.

*Ali: When is your book going to be on Amazon?*

*Jack (laughing):* Whenever I'm not nearly dying, and can figure out Amazon. This year, hopefully.

*Ali: Well, let me know when it's ready because I would like to read it.*

*Jack:* I'll send you a free copy for being my therapist for two hours.

* * *

## The Future

*Ali: How do you see AI transforming the agency space?*

*Jack:* PPC agency owners were used to AI before everyone started talking about it.

When I think back to my trips to Google's head offices, I was barely out of my teenage years. Even then, they were teaching us about machine learning and algorithms and what would become AI. So we were already deploying AI. We had a budget monitoring software that would flag if we were going too fast, too slow, or if conversion rates spiked. It would then temporarily deploy extra spend and take it away later in the month. We were already very used to it and when it became more mainstream, the biggest pain for us was clients thinking they knew how to use it. We had one client who was obsessed with an AI image generator. They kept sending us stupid images they wanted us to put in the ads.. We already had the right AI in place, optimising campaigns alongside the humans. So initially the headache was keeping our clients focused and away from the shiny new toys.

Some agencies in the group I left have leaned into AI advisory, which I think is really smart. Peter and Christina Polarsi run an agency leading the charge, and they are passionate about AI. They run a two-day workshop with their clients because the education level among the general population is still extremely limited. They help them understand how to optimise their business using AI first, then they bring in the AI-powered digital marketing solutions. It's interesting.

I think people will always want to work with people to some extent. What we do changes, and when I think back to my very first days in PPC in 2006, you changed every bid with your own hands. Within a few years, that was done by machines. Then, machines were writing the ads. Then they were designing banner ads, and now they're spitting out an entire landing page and deciding all kinds of things. Yet our value never diminished. I think that's proven by our having had 5 consecutive record-breaking years.

So it's a long-winded answer, but I think you have to adapt and be tuned in to what clients need. You've got the base skills, you've got the communication skills, you've got the tech skills, you understand AI better than probably most clients. So, just listen and react.

One commercial regret I've always had is that we gave away a lot for free. I know that's ridiculous because earlier I said our entire purpose is to help people, but I mean we were basically fractional CMOs for our clients at some points because they had so many problems in their business. Our ads would not have worked if we hadn't helped them. So we always fixed a bunch of stuff and gave a bunch of advice that they really should have been paying a better CMO to do.

I think going forward it's about making sure you get paid for your consulting because in the past the product paid so well; you didn't really have to charge for your advice. Now the product is commoditised. So you've either got to build a system no one else has and sell it at a good price, or charge for the collective brainpower of your team. That would be my few cents. But honestly, I don't have a clue, and I feel kind of glad that I'm out of the game at this point. I think so many people say, 'This is dead!', 'This is the next big thing!' but our industry doesn't pivot overnight. So, as long as you don't completely miss the bus and ignore something for 3 years after a clear shift, you'll probably be okay. Especially if you're a healthy business with a diverse client risk profile, lots of cash, and a good pipeline. If you have to change your value prop once a year for the next three years while the world changes, so be it. Figure it out.

*Ali: What is your best piece of advice for agency owners?*

*Jack:* Let go of your Lego and find the thing that lights up your soul. For me, it was public speaking and looking after my team. That's ultimately why I was so heartbroken. I never wanted to leave them. In my first 5 years, I did everything - 24-hour days, building landing pages, websites, contracts, new business - the lot. But once I got to a point where I could start letting go of my Lego and stepping away from things like sales, I had the time to discover myself and have fun.

I think people forget we should aspire to surround ourselves with good people and do stuff that makes our hearts flutter a bit in a good way. We should learn new stuff and do what serves our souls. I can tell you that on my worst days in hospital, when I had to go back into emergency surgery less than a day after the first one - I wasn't thinking about my agency. None of it mattered. Yet I have lived a great life, and I believe that's because I did what served my soul. If you're not happy at work, you will not be happy at home. You're going to be a miserable git. You will not be a good husband or wife or dad or mum. This thing has such an enormous impact on your life, and if you don't do it well, and you don't make it serve your soul - it might ruin your life.

You might say, 'Well, you still nearly ruined your life because it nearly killed you'. It didn't nearly kill me. It was my ignoring my health for 5 years that nearly killed me. I don't think success and health are mutually exclusive, but you have to make better choices than I did.

*Ali: It there anything I've missed? Any final thoughts you would like to add?*

*Jack:* You haven't missed anything because you're the perfect host. But, I think one thing I want to articulate is that I don't think there's anything wrong with exiting an agency, but I think you should be clear about it. Circumstances can change, and maybe you thought you wouldn't, and then you did, but personally, I never felt comfortable even considering offers that came along because the team bought into my vision. I don't understand how you can run a 10-year plan and vision with your team and then just take an offer and run off to the bank unless you've been upfront about it.

If you're starting an agency and you're like, 'Right, guys, get in on the ground floor. We're going to scale this thing and sell it, and everyone's going to get a piece'. That's completely different and fine. For me, it was the emotional attachment. That's ultimately why I didn't want to go. I think if anyone who reads this doesn't relate to that attachment, they just don't have a very good team. That is the truth. If you don't find the idea of leaving your team heartbreaking, you just haven't found the right team yet. And when you do: a) it'll break your heart when you have to leave them, and b) you'll probably 5x your growth because they will bring out the best in you. People think about their team as production powerhouses and in terms of high billers and utilisation rates, but I think the best team in the world brings out the best in the founder. With that, I will end my sermon.

*Ali: It's true that your team is at the heart of it all. It's something I struggle with when I talk about The Agency Growth Pad. To carry my message, I talk about how I built the first sales team to double the agency's size and release the founder to work on M&A. Which is true, but I know, and feel very acutely, that I didn't do that on my own. I did it together with my team.*

*Jack:* Even having that feeling is proof you're a good leader, right? The cognisance that you did nothing on your own is wonderful. I didn't actually ask you this in the first meeting, so I'm going to ask it now. Why are you writing this book, and why are you talking to people like me?

*Ali: I get to speak to people like you and to hear about the massive journey that you've been on. But also I'm writing it because the agencies I work with want to make their business more stable – potentially to exit, potentially just to get more sleep at night. The journey from a chaotic agency owner's life to a founder-independent business can feel mysterious. So, I want to demystify it and inspire owners by painting that picture in different ways because I think every agency is unique.*

*Jack:* It's true, and I bet you we've all contradicted each other.

*Ali: So what's next for you?*

*Jack:* Uh, lots of doctor's appointments. I'm still in that cycle of trying to get fully better, which I have to continue doing.

I get a real kick out of helping people, even if it's putting up shelves for Lisa. When I get my 'good boy,' for doing that, it makes me so happy. Helping other people and getting a bit of thanks for it makes me really, really happy, so I will continue to do that. I also had a bit of a revelation post-therapy and post-COVID, which was that I enjoy writing. So, I've been working on books. I'm also working on a bizarre, eccentric writing project. I'm not trying to tease it. I'm just telling you that my wife thinks I'm completely mad.

*Ali: I have to hear more about this!*

*Jack:* I might tell you offline, but not while the buttons are on. The point is I'm just having fun. When I feel physically fine and I'm out of the woods and cleared by doctors, I will most likely do something like you are and become an adviser to other agency owners. Ideally, I can find Jacks and Jackies, who are versions of me 5-10 years ago, and I can save them a bit of pain, a bit of health, and a bit of mental health.

Crohn's is a lifelong disease, and I've survived these couple of rounds of surgeries this year, but I obviously have to be very mindful going forward about what I commit myself to. So at most I will release a book or two a year and advise people maybe two days a week.

## Finding Jack Porter-Smith

You can find Jack's book '*Sixty Seconds of Glory: Selling From The Stage For Wildly Predictable Agency Growth*' on Amazon. Jack also later revealed that his other project is his memoir called, '*Writing Home*'.
You can find Jack on LinkedIn at: linkedin.com/in/jackportersmith/

* * *

> **Want to see how exit-ready your agency is?**
> *Take the 3-minute test:* ***agencyexits.co.uk/book***
>
> **Not selling yet?**
> *Now is a great time to build for the future.*
> *Book a call and I'll show you how to scale profitably, reduce founder dependency, and build a high-value agency on your terms.*
> ***agencyexits.co.uk/contact***

* * *

## Exit Story Takeaways

**1. Exit-readiness is risk management**

Jack never wanted to leave, but health forced his hand. Because the business was profitable, cash-rich, and structurally sound, he had options. Even if you don't plan to sell, build as if you might have to tomorrow. Exit-readiness isn't always about selling; it's also about creating resilience so that if something unexpected happens, you have options.

**2. Education is the best new business machine**

Jack's most effective marketing wasn't slick campaigns or funnels; it was teaching. Speaking, writing, and sharing knowledge made Utopiads visible and trustworthy. Founders who educate their market often find they don't need to chase leads and that the leads start chasing them.

**3. Even good leadership needs to evolve**

Jack was always a thoughtful, values-led leader. But as the agency grew, so did the emotional and cultural needs of the team. He spoke candidly about moments where feedback stung, but helped him grow. Buyers look for signs that a business has clear leadership and a strong, connected culture - and that doesn't happen by accident.

**4. Know what lights you up and what drains you**

Jack's most joyful years came after he let go of tasks that drained him and focused on what energised him: speaking, team culture, and education. That shift didn't just serve him; it also made the business stronger and gave his team opportunities to grow.

**5. Founders need somewhere else to place their identity**

Like many, Jack had wrapped his identity up in the agency. Exiting meant working out who he was without it and dealing with the sense of grief that was left behind. That's a quiet, important part of the exit journey - and one worth thinking about before the papers are signed.

# 11

# It's Money or Your Life, Isn't It?

*"I felt we'd created an ethos that I wanted to preserve, and I now look back and realise that is ego bullshit; it's just a business. Just sell it."*
*– Jon Payne*

**Entrepreneur:** Jon Payne
**Exit Type:** Abandoned Management Buyout | Buyout With Commission
**Exited Agency:** Noisy Little Monkey
**Exit Value:** Undisclosed
**Time To Exit:** 13.5 Years
**Employees At Exit:** 8
**Year:** 2023
**Purchaser:** SpiderDigital

When you first meet Jon Payne, you don't immediately think 'rigid strategist' or 'spreadsheet assassin.' You think: here's someone who genuinely *loves* SEO, loves his clients, and built an agency because he wanted to do great work with great people. Which is exactly what he and his wife, Nic, did with Noisy Little Monkey.

Nic is a skilled operator and, between them, they ran a tight, well-oiled machine: the agency was slick, professional, and profitable. Day-to-day running of the business was never an issue. But they didn't have an exit route mapped.

Building for love isn't the same as building for exit. Jon's approach was more jazz than classical – instinctive, improvised, and totally unrehearsed. So, when the time came to step away, there wasn't a neat succession plan, or a buyer lined up. There was just Jon, tired and burnt out, realising he couldn't keep running at full speed – and *definitely* couldn't stomach a gruelling earn-out.

What followed was one of the most creative exit deals I've ever seen.

Jon and Nic leaned on their network, acted on instinct, and struck a truly unusual deal that gave them freedom, financial security, and a way out on their own terms. It wasn't the highest valuation in history, but it was the right move at the right time. And most importantly, it was right *for them*.

Take this story as a cautionary tale – or a reminder that leaving it late comes at a cost. Burnout will limit your choices and cause you unnecessary stress. And yet – through creativity and reputation – Jon and Nic landed on their feet.

Here's how they did it.

* * *

## The Entrepreneur

## Origins

*Ali: How did you begin your career?*

*Jon:* I used to be a shepherd. When I left school, I wanted to work with animals and be outside. I didn't go to university or college. I didn't want to be in an office. I was a shepherd for three years, and at the end of that, they said I should go to college because I was reasonably academic. But I hadn't been that academic at school, so I went to an agricultural college, and in the first term they kept telling me I was going to get a distinction. So, by the second term, I was phoning it in. I got a pass.

Animal husbandry was my major, and I had to do a project, and mine was on pigs. Because of swine flu, we had computer records for pigs, which in 1988 was unusual. For other animals there were paper records, and they didn't really matter, but because of swine flu pigs had to be traceable. You had to upload your pig information to a central government database. My project was about these two pigs and their piglets. The government database was really crappy to upload stuff to, and you had to put the information onto a floppy disc and send it in, and then they would send you the entire updated database back on another floppy disc. So, it was a lot of work for something that was less than 1.3 megabytes. It was so basic.

My dad had bought me a computer when I was about 11, and I had done little with it, but I could see the logic of this database, and its management was screwed up, so I just messed around with it. I accidentally hacked this database! You could only put specific words into it with your pig's information, and mine had a very rare disease, which I couldn't input. So I just hacked it and put that disease in, and because every time the disc went back, the entire database was updated, it ended up changing data throughout the pig system. What I had done had got noticed, and so I started getting asked to help with other stuff too.

That led me into a job at a warehouse for a multi-level marketing company, where they needed a database. A multi-level marketing company was an awful place to be, but I didn't know that until I had been there about a month - the money was good though. I fixed their database, and then there were other challenges that needed different systems to talk to the database. So I learned to make the systems connect.

From there I got into peripheral sales because I didn't want to keep doing databases, and I get bored really easily. Sales suits me because I get to learn about new things, meet new people, learn about their business and what drives them - I love all of that and I'm good at building rapport fast so there's a way to commoditise that. I really leaned into it in my mid-twenties. So by then I was a pretty disgusting human being selling IT peripherals.

I loved it and did really well. So I ended up running a sales team which at its height had seven field salespeople, including myself, and then 22 consumables salespeople selling the toners that went in the printers. My boss, Kevin, bought a domain name called freecolourprinters.co.uk. He said, 'We've overstocked these printers, so what we'll do is give away the printer', and this is effectively how all printer sales work because they're tying you into buying the toner and the paper. So he said, 'We'll give away the printer, but what we'll do is we'll take the starter ink out so that if you want to buy the starter ink, that's a tenner'. So it was a tenner to be delivered and a tenner for the starter ink, together that covers our cost for this little printer and then we'd start making money on any consumable sales.

*Ali: How did you end up starting an agency?*

*Jon:* Because I'd helped with the printer website, I thought I was a web genius. It was his idea, the whole thing. But because of that, I went and started an agency with my friend Tim. He could do Access databases because he ran a company that scrapped aircraft, and they've got a lot of parts to manage, so he was very good at Access databases. I was good at sales. So we thought all we needed was someone who could tie those two things together and build a front end. That led to us starting our first web design and marketing agency in 2000, which we called 1Emotion and billed as, 'End to End Web Enabled Solutions' - can you believe it?

We were working with people who were comfortable with their current website, but when you looked at it, you would see it was a JPEG. So we had to explain that they would never get found on Yahoo with a JPEG. I'm feeling so old.

*Ali: (no comment)*

Tim and I both ran successful businesses after that one; he still does - but together we did not do a great job. When I met my wife, I was still working with Tim, and I had no money, nor did Tim. The business wasn't making much, and we'd just made people redundant. I think we kept one employee called Liam, who is just a fucking god of a cool, collected dev. But our business was not going to make any money. My now wife, Nic, said, 'Look, if we're going to be together, you can't work seven days a week and me keep lending you money'. I kept saying, 'Well, we'll be okay in a couple of years'. She was said, 'But you won't, will you?'. So I left, which enabled Tim and Liam to run this really cool company because they didn't have another burdensome person. That's gone great guns and is a really good software company now. I have no involvement in it, but we're still great friends.

Between that and starting my agency, I worked at a website agency for 6 months. I hated it. They were negligent, if not fraudulent, and over-promised and always under-delivered. I was employed as the salesperson, and they would say to me, 'Oh you've taught us SEO; we'll do the SEO'. So I'd then sell a website with SEO, and they just wouldn't do it! I was supposed to be the salesperson, but I'd be logging in on evenings and weekends to repair what should have been being done for them - so I was doing their SEO myself in my spare time. The agency didn't like that, but we'd said we were going to do it and someone needed to get it done. Plus, if they'd made their server more secure, I wouldn't have been able to just guess the password and get into it in the first place!

It was everything I'd fought against in my previous agency, and we came close to fisticuffs. I walked out and went home to Nic, who I'd only been living with for 4 months. I said, 'I've resigned'. Nic said, 'Good. Well, if you're going to resign, we'll make a plan, because no one resigns without having another job to go to. So we'll find another job and then you can resign'. I had to tell her that I had I walked out. Tacitly resigned. And that if I went back, they'd probably call the police.

The clients I had sold knew that I was working in my spare time and getting their SEO done for them, even though it wasn't my role. So when I left, a lot of them wanted to come with me. So that's how I started my next agency. Nic pretty much funded it, but it was my business, and I put together a sales target for the first six months. I needed to turn over 28 grand in six months to make sure that I could contribute my bit to our housing. That was less than half of what Nic was earning. That then became the Web Consultancy, which we renamed Noisy Little Monkey when I realised there was a bloke in Bridgewater, near where we lived, called the Web Consultancy. I really should have thought about that, but we needed to change, so I thought I'd give it a name that makes people laugh.

## Mindset

### *Ali: What prepared you for agency life?*

*Jon:* My dad has always run his own businesses. When I was five or six, my uncle John was a market trader. He would babysit me and with my cousins we'd go to the market and help him sell meat for Terry the butcher. Well, we didn't help; mainly, we'd just be a pain in the ass behind the stall. We got used to taking cash and making change.

My dad ran a record label, and he would do gigs at the Royal Albert Hall. They'd do a big paid dress rehearsal for a choir or a band on a Thursday night. Dad would record it and then press the records on Friday to sell that evening when the show started. So, on a Friday afternoon, my whole family would be in our living room putting vinyl into gatefold album sleeves ready to sell on tables over the weekend.

My dad discovered that if an old lady paid £3 for the £2.80 record and I took the change as a blonde-headed angelic child, she'd let me keep the 20p and we made an extra 10-20% on all of my sales. So, he said, 'Jonny, you give them their change, and they'll tell you to keep it and you can have half for yourself'.

My dad was also very strategic. He'd move the table at a venue so that people almost had to bump into it to be able to get out. So he was 'conversion rate optimising' and doing 'user experience' with the flow of people! Years later when I was in a band and selling merch I would get into trouble for moving the table so that people have to squeeze by. People would slow down to squeeze through and that meant a bit of a queue would start to form, and so then people would be like, 'Oh, well, if people are buying stuff, we'll buy too'.

So, the computing stuff came from livestock, and then the sales stuff is kind of in my family and where I started.

*Ali: It's making my cheeks hurt because I've been smiling. There's a lot I can relate to with having always been an outdoorsy person and thinking I would never work in an office. My marketing role was selling shop fittings like mannequins and coat hangers. So I'd write a lot about things like where to put your table. I always thought it was funny because it was the same as learning digital marketing, but translating it into the physical environment. Some of it is wild – in some shops they'll even use different size floor tiles to encourage you to walk faster or slower, depending on whether you're in a luxury aisle or a discounted one. Niche.*

*Do you have a proudest moment from the journey so far?*

*Jon:* This is why I'm not a millionaire. It's the relationships I've built with people I have worked with and people in the wider community. We won some big clients, some awards – even a Drum award or two. But no, the real thing that I'm proudest of is the relationships.

I wasn't always the best employer – by that I mean I wasn't always a good employer or a nice one. Nic tempered a lot of my bad side because she eventually started running the agency, and I was just there to wave my arms and do stuff like this book and strategy. I love the strategy bit. One of the great things now is that I don't have to manage people. I can mentor people, but I don't have to manage them. And I'm much better at that. That's a much better relationship. If I'm managing them, I'm a terrible manager and I let them down. Early in my career, I treated them very badly.

But I'm still great friends with the people I met through Noisy Little Monkey. I see some of them really regularly, and we're mates. I think it'd be interesting to see what they think. They probably think, 'Why does he keep coming to our stuff?!'. But yeah, I love that. That's probably my proudest bit – the impact that indirectly we've had on other people and the joy they continue to bring to Nicola and me.

*Ali: I love that. One of my closest friends is my old boss, who hired me into my first paid job at a shop selling jeans. I think when you meet people through work you learn a lot about each other. You have to figure out how to navigate disagreements and things you might see very differently. It helps you to build a strong connection - particularly in high-pressure roles.*

*Jon:* Yes, particularly when you're working together in a growing business - you're going to go through some really difficult times. That cements the friendship even more. I mean, that's why all corporate training involves you having to run around and do difficult things outside of your comfort zone, because hopefully team building happens by accident.

*Ali: Do you have any regrets?*

*Jon:* I am quoting a friend here. I have quite a lot of cognitive dissonance about the way I treated people earlier in my career. I never really think about that. I never really think about regrets. Does anybody? But that's one. I mean, if you compare me to the owners of big businesses, I think I was probably quite nice. But, I was just a prick sometimes to people who were my junior when I was in my twenties. Now I look at entrepreneurs in their twenties who are far more successful than I am, and people criticise them, and I think, 'They have no idea'. Most of them, I hope, will have a gradual turn or a turning point where they go, 'Oh my god, I'm just showing off and being an idiot. I didn't realise the impact I have on people'.

*Ali: That's a very honest reflection. A lot of the founders I speak to look back on their twenties and feel the same. I think I had a lot of confidence that I could do things, and no idea that I didn't know what I didn't know yet.*

*Jon:* There's a 'before anger management Jon' and an 'after anger management Jon'. By the way, I've got nothing to be angry about. I went to a group, and there were people on that course who had every reason to be damaged and angry at the world. They had been through some really incredible stuff. I've sailed through my life. I don't know why I had anger anyway, and I'm actually now getting angry at myself for that, but that's that's another thing.

My old boss Barry used to say to me, good management is just getting people to do things they wouldn't ordinarily do. And I'm really good at that. But after week two, 'Why do I still have to tell you how to do it? How come you haven't picked this up?'. I'm not good at that. So, broadly, Nicola and Tash would do most of the people stuff, and I'd do most of the high-level leadership stuff. I'd think about where we were going, and then Tash and Nic would figure out how we would get there and with the least damage to the business, or whether it really was a good idea for us to get there anyway.

I realised people were terrified of me. Ali, you've met me. I'm what, 5'8"? And I'm not a substantial guy. I didn't realise that people who were bigger than me (because all of my friends are bigger than me) actually feared me because I was in a position of 'power'. I still put 'power' in inverted commas because I thought, 'I just run an agency and there's maybe 19 people who work here. That's not powerful. I'm not Richard Branson. I run a small agency. In fact, my wife runs it, and she allows me to come in and run about!'. But of course it's their job and I'm the boss, and so if they see me losing my temper it has an impact. There was one year that I punched three laptops to death in the office. Tash said that if I punched one more inanimate object, then I would have to go to anger management or she would resign.

There came a day when I was in really early and my dog was barking while I was trying to record a webinar and I punched the desk. My dog had been barking because someone had come in early, and that person saw me. We made eye contact, and I knew they were going to tell Tash. I'm so glad it happened. It changed the way I deal with people. I realised that when someone couldn't understand what I was asking for or wasn't getting it; it wasn't them that was making me angry; it was that I felt ashamed that I hadn't done a good enough job to prep them for the job.

* * *

## Building The Agency

### Development

*Ali: Tell us about Noisy Little Monkey.*

*Jon:* We started out as pure SEO, and the unique selling point (USP) was that we did honest SEO. Later I realised that everybody who is shit also says that, so we needed to figure that out. Our guiding light became, 'We're going to put digital charlatans out of business. So, if we can't sell you SEO because we're too expensive or the time isn't right or you're not a fit for us, we will educate you enough during the sales process that you can fire your current SEO who might not be doing a good job'.

Because we started in 2008, there were so many people who were just lying. A contact would say, 'What's this report?' and we would go, 'We can't understand it. Why would they be reporting on this stuff? It doesn't seem like it's accurate for your website. You need to leave them'. Often in my reply, I would ask how much they were paying, and if it was £50 a month or some paltry amount, I would say, 'Great. Don't do it. You're less likely to get a Google penalty, and you can buy more donuts for meetings. Do that'. They'd sometimes ask, 'Oh, what if we spent it with you?' and I'd have to explain I can't do anything meaningful for £50 a month. No one can.

Everything we did was to enable businesses to realise if they were having the wool pulled over their eyes. We produced loads of content to help people educate themselves and to help them do better. We ended up running our own conferences called Digital Gaggle, which we held in Bristol. We would get people to come from all over the world and teach. I wanted them to teach my team. And I figured that if I got a room full of 200 people who could buy their services, then they wouldn't charge me. So that's what we did.

Through educating people, we started getting bigger leads because people would realise they didn't have time to learn it all and wanted to just work with us to solve it for them. I could never get my head around it because our other USP was that we *wanted* to be fired in a year. We didn't want clients to be paying us for years and years. We had some clients who were with us for 10 years, so it didn't work - but that was our ambition. We wanted to train their team to do it so they didn't have to hire an agency. If they had a marketing function, then we felt they should hire another person or educate their team to do it better. So, we would do that, but some people stayed with us. Of course, with my commercial hat on, that's perfect. We love that! But yeah, those were our two USPs.

We started out in SEO, but we later moved into other things like HubSpot. When I used to sell printers, we had built this amazing database in FileMaker Pro, and I could never find another one that was such a good sales database. When HubSpot Marketing was released and it had a bit of sales in it, I thought, 'This is it!'. It gives us measurements. We can do quotes in it. We can track where the quote's going. We can measure revenue. We can measure revenue by tweet, by web page, etc.'

So we became a partner. They got upset with us because we didn't sell it for the first 12 months because we wanted to test it on ourselves first. It worked, so we started selling it and became a HubSpot Diamond partner. It was brilliant because we could link the sales and marketing pieces.

That then became our thing. We would educate our team to understand how business works. The big thing is that if we're dealing with a small business, then after you've spoken to the marketing manager, people come onto a call who are going to make a decision in five minutes. Because you only have five minutes, you have to get as much out of them about their personal ambition for the business and themselves very quickly so that you can explain how you can help. I worked with the team on doing that, which is why I think so many of them have gone on to do great things because, yes they're good at the marketing, sales or CRM, but actually what they're really good at is understanding the levers they need to pull on in a business to make it work.

That became a USP for us, because often you weren't talking to someone who knew about marketing; in fact, a lot of them didn't. They knew about the product or service, which meant we could focus on the stuff we were really good at which is ultra technical SEO, recovering people from Google penalties that they've got somewhere else, and building a system that converts strangers into customers and at a higher revenue per customer.

*Ali: I love that you brought commercial awareness into the team because it's so impactful for the clients. When I was researching Noisy Little Monkey, one thing that came up a few times was the 'irreverent brand voice'. How did that come about?*

*Jon:* Wow, that's cool! I just didn't want us to be the same. When we started I was reasonably new to Bristol and I was getting hired by marketing agencies as their white label SEO solution, which I had to stop doing because they would say that I'd done stuff, charge it at a premium rate and then I hadn't done it and people would get in touch with me on LinkedIn and go, 'This doesn't seem to be getting results,' and I would have to say, 'That's because I haven't worked for you for six months!'.

Lots of agencies are named after the founders with something like three initials and then 'creative', there's lots of that. There was also a lot of boring talk. Part of the reason I'm difficult to employ is I don't want to be somewhere that's boring, and I find my own company boring. So, we deliberately went for a logo that was infantile to begin with, and Tash smartened it up because she told us, 'We cannot have this fucking monkey with a colander on its head as a logo anymore'.

That was okay when we were dealing with people who were spending £500 a month, but we'd got £5k–10k a month retainers and at board level it looks weird. We didn't change our tone of voice, but Tash knew we needed to look cooler.

We used to get leads who'd be excited about our brand voice and our creativity but who were lawyers, banks, accountants and in pharmaceuticals. They'd want it to be fun like our tone of voice, but then we'd get nothing approved. They would become a churn risk, and no one would want to work on their account because we'd repeatedly give them amazing creative ideas, and they'd be like, 'Yeah, well, no, we can't do that. So let's just do us but a bit more?'. There's a good quote; you want the famous, rich or inspired as clients. Famous because you want their logo on your website, and rich because no one knows them but they pay for all the stuff that you do that's inspiring. And so we would try to keep the balance of famous, rich, and inspired. Sometimes we would work for a charity for free because that would inspire us again, or we'd do a discount for a startup that we shouldn't work with.

The people who really inherited some of our madness and our chaos were the inspired ones who said, 'Look, just do what you want. We'll obviously have ultimate sign-off, but we really want your flavour, and we need you to give us a flavour like that.'

My mum actually came up with the name because I couldn't find a domain name. She used to quote to me that the way random works is if you get an infinite number of monkeys with an infinite number of typewriters, at some point one of them will write word for word the complete works of Shakespeare. It might take an infinite amount of time, but it'll happen. So I said, 'Mum, you remember the infinite monkeys? I don't have them, but I just need one monkey that I plug into Google to find me some keywords,' and she said, 'Well, I used to call you my noisy monkey'. That name was owned by some teenagers in Idaho who were in a band, and their musical credibility wouldn't let them sell it to me. So we went for Noisy Little Monkey, and once you have a name like that, everything becomes playful.

* * *

## The Exit

### Preparation

*Ali: Did you always think you would exit?*

*Jon:* We were thinking about selling for five or six years before we did. We had the pandemic in the middle of it. So, that knocks out two of those years. We'd gone to enough events where clever people who'd done it had said, 'You need to be thinking about it a minimum of 5 years before you do it'. What I didn't realise was that when they said 'Thinking about it', they meant more than the directors just discussing over breakfast that it would be cool.

*Ali: What were the first steps you took towards exiting?*

*Jon:* We tried to sell it to the team internally with a management buyout. Tash was very involved in the business and remains a big part of our lives. So we thought we would make her the MD, give her a shareholding and tell her she should run the company. So, we pitched it to Tash, and she said, 'No, why would I want to ruin my life? You two are stressed out of your minds all the time. I'm stressed out of my mind 50% of the time. I don't want to be any more stressed'. So we insisted that she have a shareholding anyway because we felt she was part of the family. We didn't give her any more responsibilities; we just wanted to recognise her. I know all agency owners say, 'Don't do that'. And that's good advice actually; it bit us in the arse! Within 18 months of giving her the shares, we ended up having to buy her out to sell the business, and it cost us a fuck-ton. We had paid her tax on getting the shares as well. Anyway, Tash was very happy. Well, she wasn't very happy. We just made her redundant, but she was happy with the money. So, our first step was to try to sell it internally with pretty much no warning to her either.

After we'd given her the shares, we were being approached once or twice a month by people who said they were interested. I didn't want to sell it until we were over £1 million because that had been my goal. What a prick I was sticking to this ridiculous goal of being over £1 million, which we had! But because I only look at gross profit, I didn't notice we'd gone over it. About a year later I asked Nic why she hadn't told me, and she said, 'Well you only look at gross profit!'. So, that shows you what a great manager I was. So then we started talking to some of those people, and I just hated it.

We loved our team, and we didn't want to just give them to anybody because we didn't want to ruin their lives. Dick move. Their lives would not have been ruined, and we could have taken much more money.

That's my key learning, that their lives would have been fine, because we sold it and their lives are still fine. In fact, we made more of them miserable by making them redundant first. We could have sold it when it was a bit more profitable before the pandemic if we hadn't been so worried about them. I felt we'd created an ethos that I wanted to preserve, and I now look back and realise that is ego bullshit; it's just a business. Just sell it.

So while we were getting interest from acquirers, and I was resisting them, we hired an operations director to make her managing director in the future. We thought, 'Brilliant, we'll just step back and we actually won't sell it'. The new operations director, Charlie, was previously the general manager of one of our competitors, and she was friends with our marketing manager, Claire. So she would just come around on a Friday and be pissed off that we hadn't closed the office at 4 so that they could go to the pub. So when she started with us, her first thing was, 'Right, we don't work past 4 on a Friday. That's fucking savage. You're an agency. People go for a drink at 4'. I was still thinking that we were a different kind of agency and she put her foot down and said that it was the new rule. Obviously, everybody loved it.

Charlie didn't quite work out. I've never really questioned her about it because I love her so much and I don't want the answer to be that she didn't want to work with us - and I think that's the answer. She got offered a better job, with more money, working with people from PwC and Ernst & Young. At the time I was livid, but I understood. She left after six months, and she'd rebuilt the business in her image, so we then had to rebuild it back into ours because we couldn't work those fucking spreadsheets!

After that, we realised Nic hadn't wanted to do it for a few years. She was committed and really loves coaching people. So she was coaching the staff and loved that, but for the rest of it? Her heart wasn't really in it. We were coming out of the pandemic, and we were building up to being £1 million again, but it was just much harder. We'd said yes to some clients we should have said no to because we needed to keep the lights on, and we'd lost 70% of our retained revenue in the first two months of lockdown, and before that we had been 98% retained. We haemorrhaged cash paying people and then laid some people off. We got to the end of that, and we were tired. Suddenly the light bulb went on one day when Nic and I were having a conversation. I said, 'I don't know why we're doing this. I don't care whether we become a £1 million or £2 million agency. I just want out'. You could see on her face the realisation, 'There goes our five-year plan because he's just mentally resigned from this job'.

So I called a person who we'd had a conversation with before the pandemic, who'd been ready to offer me quite a lot of money, and said, 'Let's start talking about you buying this business'. They ran a business that was adjacent to ours, and someone cleverer than me once said not to sell your business to someone who does the same thing because they'll be able to see all the problems with it. Sell it to someone who doesn't do the same thing but wants to bring that on as a new department. The business was beautifully run by Nic, and they'd have been able to see any problems the same as any other agency. Our accountant showed them things but felt they weren't really needed because everything was all up to date and the six-month projections looked amazing - so all the operational stuff was great.

I met with a few other potential acquirers, and I couldn't see a way to avoid an earn-out. I'd hit the wall. So we had some conversations where I said, 'I can probably do six months, but I don't want to work for me, so I definitely don't want to work for you. It can't be profit-related because if I get angry about that profit-related stuff, I'm going to fuck shit up and deliberately sabotage it for all of us because I'm done. I've got nothing'. I hadn't realised quite how spiritually and emotionally burned out we were.

So after speaking to some others, we eventually went back to the first company I had called and said, 'Should we do this deal?'. They bought it for an amount that I can't disclose, but it was very low.

Alongside this, we negotiated commission for the lifetime of all the clients we passed on and all the HubSpot commission we got. We hadn't sold a lot of HubSpot because often clients already had it and we fixed it, but there were a few that secured us lifetime commission on the clients we gave them.

*Ali: That's a very creative and unusual deal. What made you think of it?*

*Jon:* I'm in sales, so I'm used to someone bringing me a lead as a referral and saying, 'Can I pay your company to say thank you for this? Or if I can't pay them, can I pay you? Do you do your own taxes? If I can't do that, can we donate it to a charity? If you don't want to do that, can I just send you lots of wine?'. I'm used to that transactional thing. Everybody I was talking to said there's no way they were going to stick to it. And I was thinking, 'Yeah, well there's no way I'm getting through an earn-out and we'll write a contract'. The buyers seemed trustworthy, so we did a really unusual deal.

In the first year, Nic and I earned more on commission than we'd earned any other time running an agency for 15 years, and we did not do a stroke of work. It was glorious. We're still getting commission, and it's gone down over time because our staff left and therefore the clients left, but it covers all our bills.

When I was deciding whether to do the deal, I went back to my friend Tim from our first agency because he's such a clever guy. He's so empathetic, and he really understands business, but is also not so ambitious that he wants to claw his way to the top of every pole. I love him dearly. He said to me, 'Well, it's money or your life, isn't it? Why don't you just have a life? You could stay on. Maybe you hit the earn-out targets and get £3 million at the end of it – but also, maybe you don't'. I knew that there was the potential of being blocked from achieving the earn-out targets, and I just couldn't do it for two more years. So I took the deal because it gave me a runway.

I wouldn't change it. That's the weird thing, because I'm middle class now, of course I want more money and I want to spend it on shit I don't need. But actually what I've got is a brilliant relationship with my wife, which we didn't have when we were running an agency together. We broadly hated each other for 15 years, but we stayed together because no one else would have us – well, no, plenty of people would have taken Nic but certainly not me! Now we have a great relationship that's not fraught from running an agency together – you can't turn that shit off.

I also have my health. My health was fucked, and I was due for a heart attack, I suspect. My blood pressure was through the roof. My cholesterol was through the roof. I wasn't eating or living healthily. I didn't sleep well. Drank way too much coffee – like 14 to 15 cups of espresso a day. Now I'm much happier, and I love working with the clients that I've got.

*Ali: How did you tell the team what was going on?*

*Jon:* The team already knew. We thought we were going to announce it to them. My dear friend, whom I will not name, saw an email on my desktop when I had forgotten to lock it. I'd started locking my desktop a little while before, and everybody started wondering, 'Why does he do this when he gets up now?'. I never used to, so they'd seen the change in my behaviour.

While I was making a coffee, they had seen an email that was quite innocuous. It was from another agency owner saying something like 'Keen to chat to you about the business'. But we had trained them on how businesses worked, so she then told someone else and together they had their own little pow-wow. And so after a week of their knowing, we found out that they already knew. None of them had told us, and they were all fine and behaving themselves. But as soon as we found out that they knew, we had to tell them - before we had done the deal. We shared things like, 'We're going to confirm the rumours. We're planning to do it. This is where we are. These are the people we're planning to sell to. Once we've done the deal, they're coming in to meet you and to present to you what's going to happen. You can resign now, but it's probably better to wait and see if they make you redundant. All your clients are coming with you'.

We told everyone except poor Steve. Everybody would come into the office pretty regularly, but Steve, who'd been with us for 10 years, hadn't been in the office, and no one was putting anything on the phones in case we saw it. So, he didn't know there were any rumours. He was the longest-serving employee by then and an incredible SEO. So unintentionally we'd fucking pulled the rug. It was horrible, and we didn't realise. If I'd have known, I'd have taken him out for lunch first and said, 'Steve, this is what's happening. These are all the plans in detail. And by the way, Nic's written it up. Here's the printout; read it, tell us what you think, and we can go through it in the next couple of days'. But we didn't. I just assumed he knew, and it made an ass out of all of us. He was also having another baby, and his wife was having an operation after she'd had the baby. So he said, 'To be honest, there's nothing I can do about it anyway, is there?'. He stayed there three or four months and then he called me about walking away and taking a client with him. That client had always loved him from the moment they had met him. The client called and asked me, 'Will it really impact your deal badly?'. And I said, 'You know, I love the guy. He's got to come and work for you. Yes, it's going to impact my deal badly, but it needs to happen'. So, it all worked out in the end, but I felt guilty about that, actually.

## Reflections

*Ali: Did you feel any grief after the sale was done?*

*Jon:* No, Nic did, and I think she still feels the loss occasionally because she was so important to so many people's lives. When we ran Digital Gaggle, we were training thousands of people, and we did worldwide webinars for HubSpot. We had influence, and I think for Nic, she places her value on the impact she had on our employees' lives. So she felt it really keenly at first, and she had to deal with me when I was just miserable and didn't realise it for a year.

Whereas I danced through the streets when it was done. I revelled in selling shit from the office at car boot sales. I absolutely loved it. I don't think I've felt a moment's grief. I know now that I was burnt out then. I slept a lot, which I guess could have been some sort of grief, but I don't think so - I think I was just exhausted. I just fell into watching YouTube, slept a lot, ate a lot of pork scratchings, and drank a great deal - which I suppose sounds like grief, but I was delighted to be doing that. I was just so happy and remain so.

I can't believe the deal we got, and I love that this is now my life. In the end, Noisy Little Monkey was really difficult, but that's because we were trying to hide the truth from people that we really cared for because we needed to get the deal done before we could tell them we were selling. That was the really difficult bit.

*Ali: What are the key lessons you took from the sale?*

*Jon:* We could have started actually talking to someone to help us prep because they wanted a year, maybe two - six months minimum. I wanted them to sell it within six weeks. So if we'd started earlier, we could have built an understanding and a sale document. I just thought if people know us, they'll buy us, and I realised I was incredibly naïve in that. And it's because we hadn't planned, so we hadn't got rid of that naivety.

I was really fortunate because in SEO there's a real community and particularly in the South West of the UK. I'm originally from Hampshire, and we don't talk to each other in Hampshire. Maybe it's changed since I left 20 years ago, but when I moved to the South West, I was stunned that people in the Co-op would talk to me.

*Ali: I left Hampshire for Devon seven years ago, and they still weren't talking then. So, I doubt it has changed much!*

*Jon:* Of course, I forgot you're from Hampshire. Yes, I think in Bristol and the South West there is a community, and although they were my competitors, we would speak about our problems. So I had relationships with lots of other local agency owners. If you know lots of owners, then some of them will exit before you, and they'll love to tell you about it because the feeling is so good once you've done it normally. So I guess that's not a learning, but something that definitely helped me.

As a practical lesson, it would be to get a second phone because you can then do all of your emails and WhatsApps about the sale on that second phone and don't take it into the office with you. Our team finding out made no difference to what happened for us, but it meant that we couldn't control the narrative and it made us more nervous.

* * *

## The Future

*Ali: There is so much change happening with AI. What do you think is in the future for agencies?*

*Jon:* It's going to be a great time for the agencies that can embrace AI in whatever way they can. And I know that's an overused answer. So, let me move on to what I see as the proper stuff. I think there'll be less brainstorming where you sit around in an agency or at the board table because you've got a new client. Usually, you'd get your best minds together to throw ideas around, or if you're a more inclusive agency, you'd ask people to have the ideas beforehand and discuss them in a format that's less combative. I don't think that these brainstorms are so necessary because you can build yourself an agent to have those ideas for you. We all just need those little ideas that kick us off onto the actual stuff. It's very rare in those brainstorms to go, 'Oh, this is the one'. Usually the value is what it triggers in others. So actually if you can begin a brainstorm with 50-100 ideas from ChatGPT - you're there. My friend runs an AI and VR agency, and the creative stuff they do is incredible. They generate 2,000 ideas in 10 seconds with AI, and then they go through and take out the worst 1990 to get to the 10 that they then embellish and take to a client, then they do the AI thing that they were going to do with that client. I think as agencies we can learn a lot from that. Just have loads of ideas.

So I think there's less of that, admittedly fun, but kind of a waste of time, stuff. You can then have your really clever people apply their weirdness and their humanity to those ideas to make them brilliant and to make them work with the strategy that you're outlining.

I think we're still a bit away from it doing a really good finished product. If you're going to create a video, you need so many fast cuts because by second three the human you prompted for has turned into a dinosaur for no reason.

I think there are also fewer excuses for poor process and as an ex-agency owner myself, I've seen lots of poor processes, and they're difficult to fix. But it's increasingly easy to join disparate systems together with a bit of technology that might be powered by AI, and you really only need a human to support that effort rather than have to do all of it.

That means that people who are in accounts can be more meaningfully deployed to better work.

*Ali: What's your advice for agency owners?*

*Jon:* My best piece of advice for anybody who's running an agency is to only work with people who bring you joy, be that customers or clients or suppliers. Cut those life-sucking pains in the ass out of your life. If they're a big customer and they're paying you lots of money, figure out a way that you can replace them with a few other customers that, maybe don't pay you as much but, can replace that finance and bring you joy.

If you've got people in your business where the fit just isn't right, maybe it was right, or maybe it was the truth is it was never right, or you don't know why you let them pass probation - get rid of them. It'll be better for them. It'll be better for you.

*Ali: What's next for you?*

*Jon:* More of what I'm doing, which is travelling while working. I feel almost guilty about that, but that's what people are ambitious to do now, isn't it? I'll continue to maintain the three or four clients that I am working on their operations and their revenue growth side of things. So, I'll continue to do that while I travel.

You know what else? This is so gross and old man-ish, and there's an almost evangelical zeal about this that I'm not happy with - but nothing is as evangelical as a new convert, right? My job now is to stay healthy. I'm at a certain age now. I've promised Nic that I will die second. We don't have any kids, so that's really all we've got. That's the deal - I've just got to outlive her, and she's lived healthy a long time, and I've been a disgusting slob. So, my job is to stay healthy, and my duties in that job are to make sure I go to the gym three times a week. I don't know who this guy is, but he's only come along since I sold the agency, so maybe he'll stick around a while yet.

## Finding Jon Payne

You can find Jon Payne at linkedin.com/in/mrjonpayne/ or listen to his podcast at 5starpod.com - the podcast about terrible Google reviews.

* * *



* * *

## Exit Story Takeaways

**1. Don't wait until you're broken**

By the time Jon sold, he was running on fumes - spiritually fried, physically done. That damaged his appetite to work through an earn-out and boxed in his options. The lesson? It's important to plan early before exhaustion sets in.

**2. Put emotions aside**

Jon was obsessed with 'protecting the team ethos' and turned down lucrative deals because of it. With hindsight, he saw things more clearly: the team would be fine, and it was their business.

**3. Play with the deal shape**

Instead of an earn-out, Jon secured lifetime commissions on clients and HubSpot licences. The headline number was smaller, but he gained freedom, health, and long-term security. Think about what you *really* want out of the exit. Sometimes, a creative deal structure is the best one.

**4. Own the story**

Jon's team found out about the sale before he told them, which created unnecessary stress for everyone. His hindsight tip is to get a second phone, keep negotiations separate, and manage the timing of disclosure carefully.

**5. Only work with energy givers**

Jon's survival rule for agency life is this: move on from those who drain you. It could be a toxic client, a difficult supplier, or team members who sap your spark. The weight of keeping them is far heavier than the pain of letting them go.

# V

# Unusual Wisdom

*Now that we've done our research together, it's time to talk about the future.*

# 12

# Becoming Unusual

*"I set out to demystify the exit journey for agency owners.*
*I didn't know that it would lead to the start of my next Unusual journey."*
*- Ali Newton-Temperley*

Only 4% of agencies ever sell. The rest close, fade away, or trap their founders in a cycle of exhaustion and diminishing returns. At this point, selling is unusual. We've seen how the instincts of a slightly odd 8-year-old were not so far off - put energy into it, structure it, sell it. Although these instincts were ill-advised in selling tea to neighbours, there is truth to it. Now the challenge is to take what you've learned and apply it.

It's easier said than done. Agencies are hard businesses to run. Everything relies on herding people, whether that's your own team or your clients - and it can be exhausting, and at times, lonely. The vast amounts of energy it took you to get to this point, may have left you a little flat for the final furlong, but I hope that the stories you have read in this book have inspired you and to cement that you need a plan

- even if you don't intend to sell.

When I started writing, I thought it would be a project about other people's stories. What I didn't expect was how much it would change my own. My mission has always been to help agencies grow. Through writing *Agency Exits*, I met Luke Tobin, (you remember him, right?) an extremely successful founder who has built and sold two agencies and is now an investor on his own mission to help more agencies access capital, infrastructure, and consultancy that unlocks higher-value exits.

It quickly became clear that our missions were two halves of the same whole. Growth without exit planning leaves value on the table, and exit planning without growth will fail. Together, we could see the complete map in front of us.

It's called **Unusual Group** - a collective to help agencies grow and exit on their own terms. It brings together a community of ambitious founders, consultancy to sharpen positioning and systems, access to capital, and proven frameworks for preparing for sale. The model is truly unique in our industry and is built on absolute alignment among all of us, so we win together.

If you've made it to this page, you're already unusual. You're one of the few who've taken the time to step back, learn from others, and begin planning for the future.

Right now, only 4% of agencies make it. That's not enough. We're changing that.

Join us in doing something Unusual, together.

## Start Planning Today

**Want to talk about your exit?**

*Whether you're looking to make a move in the next 6-months, or ten years from now, let's talk about your plan.*

***agencyexits.co.uk***

**Want to see how exit-ready your agency is?**

*Take the 3-minute test:* ***agencyexits.co.uk/book***

# 13

# Lessons from Agency Exits

Across these pages you've heard from founders who have built, scaled, and sold agencies on their own terms. Each story carries different circumstances, but the patterns are clear. Success leaves clues.

What follows are the hard-won lessons from those exits, combined with my experience of growing agencies, and Luke Tobin's track record of helping agencies sell. Together with our team at Unusual Group, we've distilled these into a set of principles that apply whether you're preparing to sell in the next 6 months, or the next 5 years.

Taken together, these lessons form a playbook for building a high-value agency and exiting on your terms. To start your planning today, visit agencyexits.co.uk.

## Foundations & Positioning

*1. Start with the buyer.*

Your ICP isn't just your clients; it's also who will one day buy your business. Decide early who your ideal acquirer is and what they're looking for. Buyers want to take as little risk as possible. Keeping your sights on that will help you make decisions that build value in their eyes.

2. *Focus. Hard.*
Positioning is everything. Bad-fit briefs, energy-vampire clients, and 'just this once' projects drain profit and erode confidence. Choose your clients with intent and protect your margins.

3. *Productise for margin.*
Services are hard to scale. Packages can be easier. Scope, price, deliver, repeat. Margin is what buyers measure, so treat it as the core product and create something that's easy for a team to navigate so you're not the only person who can sell.

4. *Build a sellable profile.*
PR, a strong brand, and a clear tone of voice make you look like an attractive asset. Don't sound like every other agency. Buyers notice who makes waves and who blends in.

5. *Choose fortune over fame.*
Big-name logos flatter the ego, but often drive a hard bargain and come with difficult payment terms. What really counts is a balanced client mix: retainer-heavy, diversified, and profitable.

6. *Know what you stand for.*
Agencies with a point of view attract better clients, stronger talent, and more serious acquirers. A clear mission makes you magnetic. If you don't stand for anything, you'll fall into the quagmire of 'sameness'.

7. *Leverage your network.*
Peers, mentors, and industry connections are often the bridge to acquirers. Nurture that network before you need it.

## Sales & Pipeline

*1. Keep the pipeline flowing.*
Referrals and your network will only take you so far. A predictable stream of leads is the lifeblood of an agency. Those leads and sales can't all rely on you, because without them, the agency stalls and evaporates.

*2. Systemise sales.*
A founder closing deals is fragile, because the business doesn't exist for long without you. Document your funnel, measure every stage, and make sure multiple people can pitch. Buyers want to see revenue that flows without you.

*3. Teach to attract.*
Education builds trust and creates inbound demand. Whether it's events, podcasts, or content, show you and your team's expertise in public. Edutainment attracts leads and strengthens your network.

## Team & Leadership

*1. Layer your team.*
Succession can't hinge on another version of you - this means simply putting a 'number 2' in place isn't enough. Grow from the bottom up, creating strong layers of delivery, management, and leadership. That's what makes the business transferable.

*2. Make the founder redundant.*
Processes, and tools should mean no single person is a bottleneck - especially you. There are people who are more skilled than you at their specialisms; get out of their way and let them get on with it. When the

founder is replaceable, the agency is valuable.

3. *Trust your team, but watch the numbers.*
Delegation only works if you stay close to the metrics. Give your people the freedom to fly, but keep a sharp eye on delivery and margin so you can adjust. Delegation is different to abdication.

4. *Incentivise leadership.*
Schemes like EMI get senior leaders invested in the outcome. When they win from a sale, they'll drive performance with the same urgency you do.

5. *Manage communications carefully.*
Timing and confidentiality matter. Share too early, and you risk panic. Share too late and you damage trust. Handle it well, and the transition is smoother for staff, clients, and the buyer. Plus, it's less stressful for you.

6. *Build a culture that survives you.*
A team that works because of systems, clarity, and values is a team that outlasts the founder. Buyers pay more for a culture that isn't founder-dependent.

7. *Replace yourself in stages.*
First delivery, then operations, then sales. By the time of exit, you should only handle the highest-level CEO tasks. Everything else should already belong to your team.

## Discipline & Systems

1. *Build reserves.*
Cash in the bank gives you freedom. It cushions the flat patches, funds investment, and gives you options should the unexpected happen. Manage this with upfront deposits, milestone billing, cash forecasts, and billing in advance.

2. *Track what buyers value.*
Know your numbers inside out: revenue retention, gross margin, client concentration, pipeline coverage. Live as though due diligence could start tomorrow. Your agency will be stronger for it whether you decide to sell or not.

3. *Keep shareholder agreements tight.*
Even the closest co-founders need documentation. A clear agreement avoids disputes and makes exit negotiations cleaner. Do this even if you feel you won't need to.

4. *Assemble your infrastructure.*
HR, finance, IT, and systems aren't optional overheads. They're part of what makes you look like a business, not a project. Buyers expect to see them, and you need them to grow.

5. *Leverage smart tools.*
Technology and AI are no longer optional. Automation streamlines delivery, reporting, and back-office admin, freeing your team to focus on high-value work. An agency that runs on smart systems is leaner, more profitable, and more attractive to buyers.

6. *Build your data room early.*

Don't wait until due diligence starts. Keep contracts, financials, org charts, and SOPs organised and ready. It makes the process smoother and less stressful.

## Timing & Negotiation

*1. Sell on the climb.*

The best time to sell is just before the curve peaks. Buyers pay for future growth, not for explaining a dip. Aim to sell when momentum is on your side; don't leave it to when things are tough and you're tired.

*2. Don't sell burnt out.*

Exiting in desperation weakens your hand. Buyers can smell distress, and they will make you pay for it. Go to market when you still have energy, not when you're running on empty. Start planning while you're still in love with your business.

*3. Be ready to walk away.*

Resilience is leverage. If the deal isn't right for you, be prepared to walk away. It can be scary because you don't know if you'll get one as well as that again, but you must be prepared to walk away so you're negotiating from a position of strength, not desperation.

*4. Pick cultural fit over multiple.*

The headline number matters less than the deal you can live with. Alignment on values and approach will protect your team, your reputation, and often your sanity. Particularly if you're going to continue working in the agency.

*5. Structure beats size.*

Deal terms matter more than the multiple. An elegant structure with clean cash upfront can outweigh a higher valuation tied up in risky earn-outs.

6. *Keep it confidential.*
Use a separate phone or email for M&A conversations. Protect confidentiality until the timing is right.

7. *Time team messaging.*
Communicate clearly and at the right moment. Managing the story well makes for a smoother handover for staff and clients.

## Founder Mindset & Wellbeing

1. *Build resilience.*
The exit journey is long and stressful. Resilience carries you through the flat spots, the due diligence grind, and the negotiation rollercoaster.

2. *Take care of yourself.*
Burnout kills deals. If you're exhausted, you won't negotiate well or perform through an earn-out. Look after your health as deliberately as you look after your pipeline.

3. *Prepare for grief.*
Many founders feel a deep sense of loss after selling. Don't ignore it. Plan for what you're moving toward, not just what you're leaving behind.

4. *Completion can be enough.*
You don't always have to sell. Sometimes building a business that funds

other ventures or allows you freedom is a complete, valuable outcome in itself.

*5. Work with energy givers.*
Clients, colleagues, and suppliers should energise you, not drain you. Protecting your energy keeps you in the right headspace for growth and for a good exit.

*6. Don't do it alone.*
Exiting is lonely work if you're the only one carrying it. Surround yourself with peers, mentors, and fellow founders who understand the pressures. A strong network doesn't just bring acquirers closer - it keeps you sane.

* * *

> **Want to talk exits?**
>
> *Whether you're looking to exit in the next 6 months, or in ten years, let's talk about your plan and what comes next.*
>
> **agencyexits.co.uk/**

# Glossary

**Acquirer**

The buyer of your agency. Could be a trade buyer (another agency or network), private equity firm, consultancy, or even a product company looking to add services.

**ARR (Annual Recurring Revenue)**

Revenue generated from ongoing contracts (usually subscriptions or retainers), measured across a year. A key metric for buyers because it shows predictability.

**Burnout**

The physical and mental exhaustion that comes from running too hot for too long. Burnt-out founders often sell late and on poor terms.

**Cash Flow**

The movement of money in and out of your business. Agencies don't usually die from lack of profit – they die from lack of cash.

**Client Concentration**

How much of your revenue comes from your biggest clients. Too much reliance on one or two accounts is risky and reduces valuation.

**Completion**

When an agency can run independently of its founder. Often a milestone before an exit.

**Cultural Fit**
How well a buyer's values, approach, and culture align with yours. A critical factor in protecting your team and legacy after sale.

**Data Room**
The organised hub of contracts, financials, HR docs, and systems that buyers review during due diligence.

**Due Diligence (DD)**
The deep dive a buyer takes into your business before purchase. Covers financials, legal, clients, IP, and operations.

**Earn-out**
A deal structure where part of the sale price depends on future performance, often requiring the founder to stay on. Can look lucrative but is risky if not carefully structured.

**EBITDA (Earnings Before Interest, Tax, Depreciation & Amortisation)**
A common measure of agency profitability used in valuations.

**EMI Scheme (Enterprise Management Incentives)**
A UK tax-advantaged share option scheme that allows you to give senior staff equity in the business. Used to incentivise leadership and align them to a sale.

**Exit**
The process of selling (or stepping back from) your agency. Could be a trade sale, management buy-out, PE roll-up, or even IPO.

**Exit Readiness**
The state of having your agency prepared for sale at any time, with clean financials, systems, and leadership in place.

**Founder Dependency**
When the agency relies too heavily on the founder for sales, delivery, or leadership. A red flag for buyers.

**Gross Margin**
Revenue minus the direct costs of delivery (usually staff and freelancers). Indicates how profitable your core work is.

**ICP (Ideal Client Profile)**
The type of client your agency is built to serve best. Defining this helps focus positioning and attract buyers.

**Infrastructure**
The operational backbone of an agency: finance, HR, IT, and legal. Buyers expect institutional-grade infrastructure, not DIY fixes.

**LTV:CAC Ratio (Lifetime Value to Customer Acquisition Cost)**
A metric comparing how much a client is worth over their lifetime vs. how much it cost to acquire them. Higher ratios mean healthier growth.

**Management Buy-Out (MBO)**
When your management team purchases the agency, often supported by external finance.

**MRR (Monthly Recurring Revenue)**
Revenue from contracts and retainers billed monthly. Predictable and highly valued by buyers.

**Multiple**
The number applied to your profits (usually EBITDA) to determine valuation. For example, a 6x multiple on £1m EBITDA = £6m valuation.

**Net Revenue Retention (NRR)**
The percentage of recurring revenue retained from existing clients, including upgrades and downgrades. Shows whether accounts grow or shrink over time.

**PE Roll-Up (Private Equity Roll-Up)**
When PE firms buy several agencies in the same space, combine them, and sell at a higher multiple than any one could achieve alone.

**Pipeline**
Your visible stream of potential new business opportunities. Buyers want to see predictable, well-managed pipelines.

**Positioning**
The niche you own and the audience you serve. Sharp positioning protects margin and increases valuation.

**Proprietary IP**
Unique assets such as frameworks, methodologies, or technology that can't easily be copied by competitors.

**Retainer**
An ongoing contract where a client pays monthly or quarterly for services. More stable than project work and heavily valued by acquirers.

**Runway**

How long your agency can operate before running out of cash, assuming no new revenue comes in.

**Shareholder Agreement**
A legal document that sets out how decisions, exits, and disputes between shareholders will be handled. Essential even for best friends.

**Succession Planning**
The process of building layers of management and leadership so the agency isn't reliant on one or two people.

**Valuation**
The price a buyer is willing to pay for your agency, usually based on profit multiples, growth, risk, and strategic fit.

# Your Review Matters - Can You Help?

**Thank you for reading *Agency Exits*.**

This book came from dozens of hours of interviews, early-morning writing sessions, late night editing, and wanting to help agency founders like you build, scale and sell on their terms.

Every chapter represents months of conversations and careful editing to bring you the most useful insights. I am so grateful to the interviewees who have given up their time to share their experiences with us all.

**If you found even one idea helpful, would you take a minute to leave a review on Amazon?**

**I read every single one**, and they help to **shape the books that are yet to come**.

It only takes a few clicks, but it makes an enormous difference.

To your success,
Ali

# About the Author

**Ali Newton-Temperley** is Founder of Agency Exits and The Agency Growth Pad, and Group Chief Operating Officer and Founding Partner of Unusual Group, where she helps agencies scale and sell. She has lived the highs and lows of agency life, including doubling one to 80+ staff, leading its international expansion, and building its first sales team to free the founder for acquisitions. Ali specialises in sustainable, system-led growth by uniting marketing, sales and operations into one engine. With a background in psychology, counselling, marketing, sales and the arts, she brings an *Unusual* perspective to agency growth. Her book, *Agency Exits*, demystifies the journey from stressed-out owner to successful sale.

**You can connect with me on:**

- https://agencyexits.co.uk
- https://agencygrowthpad.com
- https://linkedin.com/in/aliagencygrowth

Printed in Dunstable, United Kingdom

68307353R10147